easy to make!
Pies, Pies, Pies

Good Housekeeping

easy to make!
Pies, Pies, Pies

COLLINS & BROWN

First published in Great Britain in 2008
by Collins & Brown
10 Southcombe Street
London W14 0RA

An imprint of Anova Books Company Ltd

The Good Housekeeping website is
www.goodhousekeeping.co.uk

1 2 3 4 5 6 7 8 9

ISBN 978-1-84340-442-2

A catalogue record for this book is available from the British
Library.

Reproduction by Dot Gradations Ltd
Printed and bound by SNP Leefung, China

This book can be ordered direct from the publisher. Contact the
marketing department, but try your bookshop first.

www.anovabooks.com

NOTES

- Both metric and imperial measures are given for the recipes. Follow either set of measures, not a mixture of both, as they are not interchangeable.
- All spoon measures are level.
  1 tsp = 5ml spoon; 1 tbsp = 15ml spoon.
- Ovens and grills must be preheated to the specified temperature.
- Use sea salt and freshly ground black pepper unless otherwise suggested.
- Fresh herbs should be used unless dried herbs are specified in a recipe.
- Medium eggs should be used except where otherwise specified. Free-range eggs are recommended.
- Note that certain recipes, including mayonnaise, lemon curd and some cold desserts, contain raw or lightly cooked eggs. The young, elderly, pregnant women and anyone with an immune-deficiency disease should avoid these, because of the slight risk of salmonella.
- Calorie, fat and carbohydrate counts per serving are provided for the recipes.

Picture Credits
Photographers: Craig Robertson; Nicki Dowey (pages 35, 37, 38, 40, 42, 50, 53, 56, 70, 71, 79, 82, 95, 98, 110, 111); Lucinda Symons (page 26)
Stylist: Helen Trent
Home Economist: Joanna Farrow

Contents

Foreword

Baking your own pies is surprisingly quick and easy. Shortcrust pastry, the basis of many pies, is simple to whiz up and uses everyday ingredients – flour, butter and water or egg – that you'll have to hand already. If you've never attempted to make it before, flick to the introduction where we've given tips and tricks for the shortest, lightest, crispest results, including baking blind, so the pastry doesn't turn out soggy. Step by step photographs show techniques for lining tart and pie tins, plus topping, sealing and finishing to ensure perfect results if you're making a covered pie.

It's not just shortcrust that makes a great pie. Light filo pastry cooks to a crisp and stars in vegetarian spinach and feta pie. If you fancy something more indulgent, plump for puff pastry: Camembert and tomato tarts make a great midweek supper or dinner party starter served with a peppery watercress and rocket salad.

These recipes, plus many more, from steak and kidney pie to pear and cranberry strudel, are among the many ideas featured in this book. All the recipes have been tried, tasted and cooked three times to make sure they look and taste delicious the very first time you make them.

Emma

Emma Marsden
Cookery Editor
Good Housekeeping

The Basics

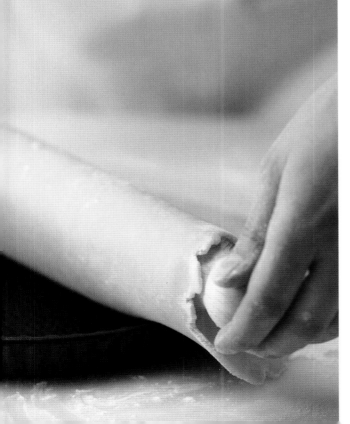

Weighing and measuring

Scales

Accurate measurement is essential when making pastry. The most accurate scale is the electronic type, capable of weighing up to 2kg (4½lb) or 5kg (11lb) in increments of 1–5g. Buy one with a flat platform on which you can put your own bowl or measuring jug, and always remember to set the scale to zero before adding the ingredients.

Measuring jugs

These can be plastic or glass, and are available in sizes ranging from 500ml (18fl oz) to 2 litres (3½ pints), or even 3 litres (5¼ pints). Have two – a large one and a small one – marked with both metric and imperial measurements.

Measuring cups

Commonly used in the US, these are used for measuring liquid and dry ingredients. Cups are bought in sets of ¼, ⅓, ½ and 1 cup. A standard 1 cup measure is equivalent to about 250ml (9fl oz).

Measuring spoons

Useful for the smallest units, accurate spoon measurements go from 1.25ml (¼ tsp) to 15ml (1 tbsp).

Getting started

You don't need much specialist equipment for making pies and tarts; in fact, you probably have many of these items in your kitchen already.

Mixing

Bowls

For making pastry by hand and mixing large quantities, such as pie fillings and toppings, you will need several large bowls.
- Plastic or glass bowls are best if you need to use them in the microwave.
- Steel bowls with a rubber foot will keep their grip on the worksurface.

Bakeware

As well as being thin enough to conduct heat quickly and efficiently, bakeware should be sturdy enough not to warp when heated. Most bakeware is made from aluminium, and it may have enamel or non-stick coatings.

Pie tins and tart tins You should have both single-piece tins and loose-based tins for flans and pies.

Pie dishes Buy a range of sizes and depths. It's also useful to have ones that are both oven- and freezer-proof, for freeze-ahead cooking.

Baking sheets It's a good idea to place tins and dishes on a large baking sheet to catch any filling that might bubble out during baking.

Electrical equipment

Food processor For certain tasks, such as making pastry or for chopping and slicing large quantities of vegetables, fruit or nuts, food processors are unbeatable. Most come with a number of attachments – dough hooks, graters and slicers – which are worth having, even if only for occasional use.

Freestanding mixer An electric mixer may be a good investment if you do a lot of pastry-making, but decide first whether you have space in your kitchen. They are big and heavy to store.

Electric hand mixer Useful for creaming together eggs and sugar for custards, meringues and ice creams, and whisking eggs or cream for fillings and toppings. They don't take up a lot of space and can be packed away easily.

Other useful utensils

Baking beans (or uncooked rice)	Non-stick baking paper
Cake slice	Palette knife
Cooling racks (two)	Pastry brush
Dredger	Pie funnel
Fine sieve	Rolling pin
Icing bag and piping nozzles	Ruler
Large metal spoon	Serrated knife
Microplane grater	Vegetable peeler
	Wire whisks

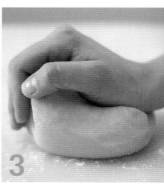

Making pastry

Shortcrust, sweet, puff and flaky pastry are the four most frequently used pastries and are delicious when home-made. Shortcrust is the simplest to prepare. Choux pastry needs more attention, while filo pastry is probably best bought ready-made.

Shortcrust Pastry

To make 125g (4oz) pastry, you will need:
125g (4oz) plain flour, a pinch of salt, 50g (2oz) unsalted butter, cut into small pieces, 1 medium egg yolk.

1 Sift the flour and salt into a bowl and add the butter. Using your fingertips or a pastry cutter, rub or cut the butter into the flour until the mixture resembles fine breadcrumbs.

2 Using a fork, mix in the egg yolk and 1½ tsp water until the mixture holds together; add a little more water if necessary.

3 Gather the dough in your hands and knead lightly. Form into a ball, wrap tightly in clingfilm and chill for at least 30 minutes before using. (This 'relaxes' the pastry and prevents shrinkage when it is baked.)

Sweet Shortcrust Pastry

Make as for shortcrust pastry (above), adding 50g (2oz) caster sugar and 2 medium egg yolks at step 2.

Using a food processor

1 You can make shortcrust or sweet shortcrust using a food processor. Put the dry ingredients into the food processor and pulse quickly to mix. Cut the butter into small pieces and add. Process until the mixture resembles breadcrumbs – do not over-process.

2 Add the egg yolk(s) and a little water if necessary, and pulse until the mixture just comes together. Continue as step 3 for shortcrust (above).

Puff Pastry

This is best made a day ahead.

To make 450g (1lb) pastry, you will need:
450g (1lb) strong white bread flour, a pinch of salt, 450g (1lb) butter, chilled, 1 tbsp lemon juice.

1 Sift the flour and salt into a bowl. Dice 50g (2oz) butter and flatten the rest into a 2cm (³⁄₄in) thick slab. Rub the diced butter into the flour. Using a knife, stir in the lemon juice and about 300ml (¹⁄₂ pint) cold water to make a soft elastic dough.

2 Knead on a lightly floured surface until smooth. Cut a cross through half the depth. Open out the 'flaps'.

3 Roll out the dough, keeping the centre four times as thick as the flaps.

4 Put the slab of butter in the centre and fold the flaps over it. Gently roll out to a rectangle measuring 40.5 x 20.5cm (16 x 8in).

5 Mark off three equal sections from top to bottom. Fold the bottom third of the pastry up over the middle and the top third down. Wrap in clingfilm and chill for 30 minutes (or freeze for 5–10 minutes).

6 Repeat the rolling, folding, resting and turning four more times, ensuring the folded edges are to the sides each time. Chill for at least 30 minutes before baking.

Quantities

Tart tins vary in depth, which affects the quantity of pastry needed. The following quantities are approximate.

Tart tin size	Quantity of pastry
18cm (7in)	125g (4oz)
20.5cm (8in)	175g (6oz)
23cm (9in)	200g (7oz)
25.5cm (10in)	225g (8oz)

Rough Puff (Flaky) Pastry

Rough puff doesn't rise as much as puff pastry but is quicker to make.

To make 225g (8oz) pastry, you will need:
225g (8oz) plain flour, a pinch of salt, 175g (6oz) butter, 1 tsp lemon juice.

1 Sift the flour and salt into a bowl. Cut the butter into 2cm (³⁄₄in) cubes and add to the flour. Mix lightly to coat the butter with flour. Using a knife, stir in the lemon juice and 100ml (3¹⁄₂fl oz) water to make a soft elastic dough.

2 Turn out the dough on to a lightly floured worksurface and knead until smooth. Roll out to a rectangle measuring 30.5 x 10cm (12 x 4in). Mark off three equal sections from top to bottom. Fold the bottom third over the middle and the top third down. Press the edges with a rolling pin to seal. Wrap in clingfilm and chill for 30 minutes (or freeze for 5–10 minutes).

3 Repeat the rolling, folding, resting and turning five more times, ensuring the folded edges are to the sides each time. Chill for 30 minutes before baking.

Choux Pastry

This soft pastry is usually spooned or piped. It contains a lot of water so it puffs up and is wonderfully light and airy.

To make eight choux buns, you will need:
65g (2$\frac{1}{2}$oz) plain flour, a pinch of salt, 50g (2oz) butter, cubed, 1 tbsp caster sugar (optional), 2 medium eggs, beaten.

1 Preheat the oven to 220°C (200°C fan oven) mark 7. Sift the flour with the salt on to a sheet of greaseproof paper. Put the butter, sugar and 150ml (¼ pint) water in a heavy-based pan over a low heat until the butter melts, then bring to the boil. Turn off the heat and tip in the flour all at once.

2 Beat thoroughly with a wooden spoon until the mixture forms a smooth ball, then transfer to a bowl and leave to cool slightly.

3 Gradually add the eggs, beating well after each addition: make sure the mixture is thick and shiny before adding more egg – if it's added too quickly the choux paste will become thin. Add just enough egg to give a smooth, glossy, dropping consistency.

4 Spoon or pipe the mixture on to dampened baking sheets and space well apart to allow room for rising. Bake for 30 minutes or as directed in your recipe.

Perfect choux

- Before you start, have all the ingredients carefully measured and in place.
- Tip all the flour into the pan at once, then leave the mixture to cool before beating in the eggs a little at a time.
- Use a dampened baking sheet (the steam will help the pastry to rise), and don't open the oven door for the first 20 minutes of baking, as the cold air will make the pastry sink. Cool the pastry completely before filling.

Using filo pastry

Making filo pastry is time-consuming, but ready-made filo is an excellent alternative. The delicate sheets of pastry are usually brushed with butter, then layered and filled to create crisp, golden treats.

1   Brush each sheet of filo pastry with cooled melted butter. Cover with another layer of filo and brush again. Repeat the layers as specified in your recipe.

Cook's Tips

Note that filo sheets vary in size depending on the brand – check whether the recipe states a specific size before buying, or buy more than stated, just in case.
Defrost filo pastry completely before you start to work with it, otherwise it may crack or crumble. The best way to do this is to leave it to thaw overnight in the refrigerator.
As you work, cover the unused sheets of pastry with a clean damp teatowel or clingfilm to prevent them from drying out and cracking.

Pastry tips and troubleshooting

The art of successful pastry making lies in measuring ingredients accurately and light, careful handling.
With the exception of choux pastry, everything needs to be kept cool – the worksurface, equipment, ingredients and your hands.
Plain flour works best, as it gives a light, crisp result - self-raising flour produces a soft, spongy pastry.
Wholemeal flour gives a heavier dough that can be more difficult to roll, so it's best to use half wholemeal and half plain flour, to lighten the texture.
Puff pastry is made using strong white bread flour – the extra gluten strengthens the dough, enabling it to withstand intensive rolling and folding. A little lemon juice is added to soften the gluten and make the dough more elastic.
Traditionally, shortcrust pastry is made with a mixture of lard (for shortness) and either butter or margarine (for flavour). If margarine is preferred, it should be the hard, block type rather than soft tub margarine.
Take care when adding the liquid to the pastry dough: too much will result in tough pastry, too little and the pastry will be very crumbly and difficult to work with. Use chilled water and just enough to bind the dough. Egg yolks are often used to enrich pastry.
The absorbency of flour varies, so use the amount of liquid stated in the recipe as a guide, adding less or more as necessary.
Mix the dough lightly and quickly, then shape into a ball and knead briefly until smooth. Over-handling will result in tough pastry, as well as warming it up. If making in a food processor, use the pulse button in short bursts until the dough just comes together.
It is important to 'rest' pastry before baking, otherwise it is likely to shrink during cooking: 'resting' relaxes the gluten in the flour. Pastries that are handled a great deal, such as puff, must be rested before and after shaping. Most pastries are rested in the refrigerator for at least 30 minutes; they need to be well wrapped in clingfilm to prevent them from drying out.
When rolling out, dust the worksurface and rolling pin with flour, never the pastry. Roll evenly in one direction only, until about 3mm ($\frac{1}{8}$in) thick, rotating the pastry as you go to give an even shape and thickness. Over-rolling, stretching and pulling will cause the pastry to shrink during baking.
A 375g pack ready-made shortcrust pastry is roughly equivalent to home-made pastry made with 225g (8oz) flour.

Lining tart and pie tins

1 Working carefully, roll out the chilled dough on a lightly floured worksurface to make a sheet at least 5cm (2in) larger than the tart tin or pie dish. Roll the dough on to the rolling pin, then unroll it on to the tin, covering it completely with an even overhang all round. Don't stretch the dough.

2 Lift the hanging dough with one hand while you press it gently but firmly into the base and sides of the tin. Don't stretch the dough while you're pressing it down.

3 For a tart case, roll the rolling pin over the tin and remove the excess dough for later use. For a pie dish, ensure the pastry covers the lip of the dish.

4 Push the dough into and up the sides of the tin or dish, so that the dough rises a little over the edge.

Baking and finishing

A light touch and a little care with rolling and lifting your prepared dough will ensure your pastry case or pie crust is crisp and perfect. It's worth taking your time for the best results.

Baking blind

Cooking the pastry before filling gives a crisp result.

1 Preheat the oven according to the recipe. Prick the pastry base with a fork. Cover with foil or greaseproof paper 7.5cm (3in) larger than the tin.

2 Spread baking beans on top. Bake for 15–20 minutes. Remove the foil or paper and beans and bake for 5–10 minutes until the pastry is light golden.

3 When cooked and while still hot, brush the base of the pastry with a little beaten egg, to seal the fork pricks or any cracks. This will prevent any filling leaking, which can make it difficult to remove the pie or tart from the tin.

Topping

Covered pies need a lid of equal thickness to the base.

1 Roll out the pastry on a lightly floured worksurface to about 2.5cm (1in) larger than the baking tin or dish. Roll on to the rolling pin, then unroll over the pie with an even overhang.

2 Using a small sharp knife, cut off the overhang just outside the rim of the pie dish.

Sealing

1 Using your thumb and index finger, pinch the base and top of the pastry dough all the way round the rim. You don't need to squeeze hard, just firmly enough to stick the pastry together. If the pie has no base, just press the top down on the rim of the tin or dish.

2 Use a fork to make decorative fluting marks around the rim.

Finishing touches

1 If you want to make decorations for the pie using leftover pastry, cut them out and put them in place, using a little water or egg glaze (see Cook's Tip) to stick them to the pastry.

2 Brush the top of the pastry with egg glaze if you like. Cut two slits in the top of the pie using a small sharp knife, to let the steam escape during baking.

Cook's Tip

Glazing pastry seals the surface and gives an attractive sheen. Brush with egg glaze (egg yolk beaten with a little water), or with beaten whole egg. Alternatively, for a less shiny finish, brush with milk.

Accompaniments

For a warming meal, mashed potatoes or – as a treat – chips are always popular with savoury pies, while on other occasions a fresh green salad fits the bill. Cream, ice cream or custard are the classic accompaniments to sweet pies and tarts.

Mashed Potatoes

To serve four, you will need:
900g (2lb) floury potatoes such as Maris Piper, 125ml (4fl oz) milk, 25g (1oz) butter, salt and ground black pepper.

1 Peel the potatoes and cut into even-size chunks. Put in a pan of cold salted water to cover, then bring to the boil and simmer for 15–20 minutes until just tender; test with a skewer or small knife. Drain well.

2 Return the potatoes to the pan and cover with a clean teatowel for 5 minutes. Alternatively, put the pan over a very low heat until all the moisture has evaporated.

3 Heat the milk in a small pan or in a jug in the microwave. Pour on to the potatoes, add the butter and season with salt and pepper.

4 Mash the potatoes until they are smooth, light and fluffy.

Chips

1 Cut the potatoes into chips and dry on kitchen paper. Heat vegetable oil in a deep-fryer to 160°C (test by frying a small cube of bread; it should brown in 60 seconds). Fry the chips in batches for 6–7 minutes until soft. Drain on kitchen paper.

2 Turn up the heat to 190°C (a cube of bread should brown in 20 seconds). Return the chips to the pan and fry until golden brown. Drain on kitchen paper, sprinkle with salt and serve immediately.

Mixed Leaf Salad

To serve eight, you will need:
3 round lettuce hearts, roughly shredded, 100g (3^1/$_2$oz)
watercress, 2 ripe avocados, roughly chopped, 1 box salad
cress, chopped, 100g (3^1/$_2$oz) sugarsnap peas, roughly
sliced, 4 tbsp French Dressing (see below)

1 Put the lettuce hearts into a bowl and add the
   watercress, avocados, salad cress and sugarsnap peas.
   Pour the dressing over the salad and toss to mix;
   serve immediately.

Variations

Instead of lettuce, use other leaves, such as rocket or
baby spinach leaves.

French Dressing

Put 1 tsp Dijon mustard, a pinch of sugar and 1 tbsp white
wine vinegar in a small bowl and season with salt and
pepper. Whisk until well combined, then gradually whisk in
the oil until thoroughly combined. Alternatively, put all the
ingredients into a screw-topped jar, secure the lid tightly
and shake vigorously to mix.

Variations

Herb Dressing: use ^{1}/$_2$ tsp mustard, replace the
vinegar with lemon juice and add 2 tbsp freshly
chopped herbs, such as parsley, chervil or chives.
Garlic Dressing: add 1 crushed garlic clove to the
dressing.
Balsamic Dressing: put 2 tbsp balsamic vinegar
into a screw-topped jar with 4 tbsp extra virgin
olive oil, salt and ground black pepper. Secure the
lid tightly and shake vigorously to mix.

Vanilla Custard

To serve eight, you will need:
600ml (1 pint) full-fat milk, 1 vanilla pod or 1 tbsp vanilla extract, 6 large egg yolks, 2 tbsp golden caster sugar, 2 tbsp cornflour.

1 Put the milk in a pan. Split the vanilla pod and scrape the seeds into the pan, then drop in the pod. If using vanilla extract, pour it in. Bring to the boil, then turn off the heat and leave to cool for 5 minutes.

2 Put the egg yolks, sugar and cornflour in a bowl and whisk to blend. Remove the vanilla pod from the milk and gradually whisk the warm milk into the egg mixture.

3 Rinse out the pan. Pour the custard back in and heat gently, whisking constantly, for 2–3 minutes. The mixture should thicken enough to coat the back of a wooden spoon in a thin layer. Remove the pan from the heat.

4 If you are not serving the custard immediately, pour it into a jug. Cover the surface with a round of wet greaseproof paper to prevent a skin from forming, then cover with clingfilm and chill for up to 4 hours. To serve hot, reheat very gently.

Perfect custard

- To avoid curdling, don't let the custard overheat during cooking.
- If you want a much thinner consistency, omit the cornflour.

Vanilla Ice Cream

1 Make the Vanilla Custard (see left), leaving the vanilla pod in the milk for 20 minutes in step 1.

2 In step 2, omit the cornflour and increase the amount of sugar to 100g (3½oz).

3 After the custard has thickened in step 3, leave to cool completely.

4 Stir 600ml (1 pint) double cream into the custard, until evenly blended. Pour into an ice-cream maker and freeze or churn until frozen. Alternatively, pour the mixture into a shallow freezerproof container, cover and freeze until partially frozen. Mash with a fork to break up the ice crystals, then return to the freezer for another 1–2 hours. Repeat and freeze for another 3 hours. Allow the ice cream to soften slightly at room temperature before serving.

Yogurt Ice Cream

This is easy to make without an ice-cream maker.

To serve six, you will need:
4 large egg yolks, 125g (4oz) icing sugar, 150ml (¼ pint) double cream, 300g (11oz) Greek yogurt.

In a large bowl, whisk the egg yolks together with the icing sugar until thick. In a separate bowl, whip the cream until it begins to thicken, then fold in the yogurt. Fold the yogurt mixture into the egg mixture, pour into a shallow freezerproof container, cover and freeze.

Melting

For cooking or making decorations, chocolate is usually melted first.

1 Break the chocolate into pieces and put in a heatproof bowl or in the top of a double boiler. Set over a pan of gently simmering water. Make sure the base of the bowl is not touching the water. Heat very gently until the chocolate starts to melt, then stir only once or twice until completely melted.

Chocolate curls

1 Melt the chocolate, as above, and spread it out in a thin layer on a marble slab or clean worksurface. Leave to firm up.

2 Use a sharp blade (such as a pastry scraper, a cook's knife or a very stiff spatula) to scrape through the chocolate at a 45-degree angle. The size of the curls will be determined by the width of the blade.

Using chocolate

As well as being a delicious ingredient in many sweet pies and tarts, chocolate can be used to make attractive decorations.

Shaving

This is the easiest decoration of all because it doesn't call for melting the chocolate.

1 Hold a chocolate bar upright on the worksurface and shave pieces off the edge with a swivel peeler.

2 Alternatively, grate the chocolate against a coarse or medium-coarse grater, to make very fine shavings.

Zesting citrus fruit

Orange and lemon zest are important flavourings in many recipes. Most citrus fruit is sprayed with wax and fungicides or pesticides. Unless you buy unwaxed fruit, wash it with a tiny drop of washing-up liquid and warm water, then rinse with clean water and dry thoroughly on kitchen paper.

To use a grater, rub the fruit over the grater, using a medium pressure to remove the zest without removing the white pith.

To use a zester, press the blade into the citrus skin and run it along the surface to take off long strips of zest.

Preparing fruit

All kinds of fruit appears in tarts and pies. A few simple techniques will make it easy to prepare both familiar and not-so-familiar fruit.

Segmenting citrus fruit

Segments of orange make a good topping for sweet tarts and can also be served alongside the dessert; they need to be prepared so that no skin, pith or membrane remains.

1   Cut off a slice at both ends of the fruit, then cut off the peel, just inside the white pith.

2   Hold the fruit over a bowl to catch the juice and cut between the segments, just inside the membrane, to release the flesh. Continue until all the segments are removed. Squeeze the juice from the membrane into the bowl and use as required.

Preparing apples

1 **To core** an apple, push an apple corer straight through the apple from the stem to the base. Remove the core and use a small sharp knife to pick out any stray seeds or seed casings.

2 **To peel**, hold the fruit in one hand and run a swivel peeler under the skin, starting from the stem end and moving around the fruit, taking off the skin until you reach the base.

3 **To slice**, halve the cored apple. For crescent-shaped slices, stand the fruit on its end and cut slices into the hollow as if you were slicing a pie. For flat slices, hold the apple cut-side down and slice with the knife blade at right angles to the hollow left by the core.

Preparing pears

1 **To core**, use a teaspoon to scoop out the seeds and core through the base of the pear. Trim away any remaining hard pieces with a small knife. If you halve or quarter the pear, remove any remaining seeds.

2 **To peel**, cut off the stem. Peel off the skin in even strips from tip to base.

3 **To slice**, halve the cored, peeled pear lengthways, then slice with the pear halves lying cut-side down on the chopping board.

4 **To make pear fans**, slice at closely spaced intervals from the base to about 2.5cm (1in) from the tip, making sure you don't cut all the way through. Press gently to fan the slices, then use a palette knife to lift the pear gently on to your pie or plate.

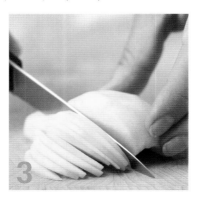

Preserving colour

The flesh of apples and pears starts to turn brown when exposed to air. If you are not going to use the prepared fruit immediately, toss with lemon juice.

Pitting cherries

A cherry stoner will remove the stones neatly, but it is important to position the fruit correctly.

1   First, remove the stems from the cherries, then wash the fruit and pat dry on kitchen paper. Put each cherry on the stoner with the stem end facing up. Close the stoner and gently press the handles together so that the metal rod pushes through the fruit, pressing out the stone.

2   Alternatively, if you do not have a cherry stoner, cut the cherries in half and remove the stones with the tip of a small pointed knife.

Stoning larger fruits

Peaches, nectarines, plums, greengages and apricots can all be prepared in the same way.

1   Following the cleft along one side of the fruit, cut through to the stone all around the fruit.

2   Twist gently to separate the halves. Ease out the stone with a small knife. Rub the flesh with lemon juice to prevent discoloration.

Peeling peaches

Peaches may be peeled for use in pies and tarts.

1   Put in a bowl of boiling water for 15–60 seconds (depending on ripeness). Don't leave in the water for too long, as the heat will soften the flesh. Put in a bowl of cold water.

2   Work a knife between the skin and flesh to loosen the skin, then gently pull to remove. Rub the flesh with lemon juice.

Preparing pineapples

1 Cut off the base and crown of the pineapple, and stand the fruit on a chopping board. Using a medium-sized knife, peel away a section of skin, going just deep enough to remove all or most of the hard, inedible 'eyes'. Repeat all the way around.

2 Use a small knife to cut out any remaining traces of the eyes.

3 Cut the peeled pineapple into slices.

4 You can buy special tools for coring pineapples but a 7.5cm (3in) biscuit cutter or an apple corer works just as well. Place the biscuit cutter directly over the core and press down firmly to remove the core. If using an apple corer, cut out in pieces, as it will be too wide to remove in one piece.

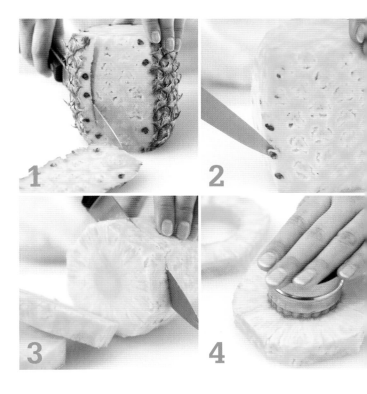

Preparing mangoes

1 Cut a slice to one side of the stone in the centre. Repeat on the other side. Cut parallel lines into the flesh of one slice, almost to the skin. Cut another set of lines to cut the flesh into squares.

2 Press on the skin side to turn the fruit inside out, so that the flesh is thrust outwards. Cut off the chunks close to the skin. Repeat with the other half.

Using passion fruit

The seeds are edible but if you want the fruit for a purée or sauce, you will need to sieve them.

1 Halve the fruit and scoop the seeds and pulp into a food processor or blender. Process for 30 seconds, until the mixture looks soupy. Alternatively, just scoop the seeds and pulp into a sieve, as step 2.

2 Pour into a sieve over a bowl and press the pulp hard with the back of a spoon to release the juice.

Hygiene

When you are preparing food, always follow these important guidelines.

Wash your hands thoroughly before handling food and again between handling different types of food, such as raw and cooked meat and poultry. If you have any cuts or grazes on your hands, be sure to keep them covered with a waterproof plaster.

Wash down worksurfaces regularly with a mild detergent solution or multi-surface cleaner.

Use a dishwasher if available. Otherwise, wear rubber gloves for washing-up, so that the water temperature can be hotter than unprotected hands can bear. Wash and change drying-up cloths and cleaning cloths regularly. Note that leaving dishes to drain is more hygienic than drying them with a teatowel.

Keep pets out of the kitchen if possible; or make sure they stay away from worksurfaces. Never allow animals on to worksurfaces.

Shopping

Always choose fresh ingredients in prime condition from stores and markets that have a regular turnover of stock to ensure you buy the freshest produce possible.

Make sure items are within their 'best before' or 'use by' date. (Foods with a longer shelf life have a 'best before' date; more perishable items have a 'use by' date.)

Pack frozen and chilled items in an insulated cool bag at the check-out and put them into the freezer or refrigerator as soon as you get home.

During warm weather in particular, buy perishable foods just before you return home. When packing items at the check-out, sort them according to where you will store them when you get home – the refrigerator, freezer, storecupboard, vegetable rack, fruit bowl, etc. This will make unpacking easier – and quicker.

Food storage and hygiene

Storing food properly and preparing it in a hygienic way is important to ensure that it remains as nutritious and flavourful as possible, and to reduce the risk of food poisoning.

The storecupboard

Although storecupboard ingredients generally last a long time, correct storage is important.

Always check packaging for storage advice – even with familiar foods, because storage requirements may change if additives, sugar or salt have been reduced. Check storecupboard foods for their 'best before' or 'use by' date and do not use them if the date has passed.

Keep all food cupboards scrupulously clean and make sure food containers and packets are properly sealed.

Once opened, treat canned foods as though fresh. Always transfer the contents to a clean container, cover and keep in the refrigerator. Similarly, jars, sauce bottles and cartons should be kept chilled after opening. (Check the label for storage time after opening.)

Transfer dry goods such as sugar, rice and pasta to moisture-proof containers. When supplies are used up, wash the container well and dry thoroughly before refilling with new supplies.

Store oils in a dark cupboard away from any heat source as heat and light can make them turn rancid and affect their colour. For the same reason, buy olive oil in dark green bottles.

Store vinegars in a cool place; they can turn bad in a warm environment.

Store dried herbs, spices and flavourings in a cool, dark cupboard or in dark jars. Buy in small quantities as their flavour will not last indefinitely.

Store flour and sugar in airtight containers.

Refrigerator storage

Fresh food needs to be kept in the cool temperature of a refrigerator to keep it in good condition and discourage the growth of harmful bacteria. Store day-to-day perishable items, such as opened jams and jellies, mayonnaise and bottled sauces, in the refrigerator along with eggs and dairy products, fruit juices, bacon, fresh and cooked meat (on separate shelves), and salads and vegetables (except potatoes, which don't suit being stored in the cold). A refrigerator should be kept at an operating temperature of 4–5°C. It is worth investing in a refrigerator thermometer to ensure the correct temperature is maintained.

To ensure your refrigerator is functioning effectively for safe food storage, follow these guidelines.

To avoid bacterial cross-contamination, store cooked and raw foods on separate shelves, putting cooked foods on the top shelf. Ensure that all items are well wrapped.

Never put hot food into the refrigerator, as this will cause the internal temperature of the refrigerator to rise.

Avoid overfilling the refrigerator, as this restricts the circulation of air and can prevent the appliance from working properly.

It can take some time for the refrigerator to return to the correct operating temperature once the door has been opened, so don't leave it open any longer than is necessary.

Clean the refrigerator regularly, using a specially formulated germicidal refrigerator cleaner. Alternatively, use a weak solution of bicarbonate of soda: 1 tbsp to 1 litre (1¾ pints) water.

If your refrigerator doesn't have an automatic defrost facility, defrost regularly.

Maximum refrigerator storage times

For pre-packed foods, always adhere to the 'use by' date on the packet. For other foods, the following storage times should apply, providing the food is in prime condition when it goes into the refrigerator and that your refrigerator is in good working order.

Vegetables and Fruit

Green vegetables	3–4 days
Salad leaves	2–3 days
Hard and stone fruit	3–7 days
Soft fruit	1–2 days

Dairy Food

Cheese, hard	1 week
Cheese, soft	2–3 days
Eggs	1 week
Milk	4–5 days

Fish

Fish	1 day
Shellfish	1 day

Raw Meat

Bacon	7 days
Game	2 days
Minced meat	1 day
Offal	1 day
Poultry	2 days
Raw sliced meat	2 days
Sausages	3 days

Cooked Meat

Pies	2 days
Sliced meat	2 days
Ham	2 days
Ham, vacuum-packed (or according to the instructions on the packet)	1–2 weeks

1

Savoury Pies and Pastries

Cook's Tip

If you don't finish the pie, it's just as delicious cold the next day or, if you prefer, warm it in the oven at 200°C (180°C fan oven) mark 6 for 15–20 minutes. Cover with foil if it starts to overbrown.

1 tbsp vegetable oil

1 onion, finely chopped

1 garlic clove, crushed

1 tbsp cumin seeds

400g (14oz) baby leaf spinach

1.1kg (2½lb) waxy potatoes, such as Desirée, boiled until tender, cooled, peeled and sliced

2 x 200g packs vegetarian feta cheese, crumbled

2 medium eggs, beaten

200g pack filo pastry, thawed if frozen

50g (2oz) butter, melted

salt and ground black pepper

Spinach and Feta Pie

1 Heat the oil in a large pan and cook the onion for 10 minutes until soft. Add the garlic and cumin and cook for 1–2 minutes. Add the spinach, cover and cook until the spinach has just wilted, about 1–2 minutes. Tip into a bowl and allow to cool. Add the potatoes, cheese and eggs. Season and mix.

2 Preheat the oven to 200°C (180°C fan oven) mark 6. Lightly butter a 28cm (11in) tart tin. Unroll the pastry and cut the sheets lengthways into three. Work with one-third of the strips at a time and cover the remainder with clingfilm. Lay a strip on the tin, starting from the middle so that half covers the tin and half hangs over the edge. Brush with melted butter, then lay another strip next to it, slightly overlapping, and brush again. Repeat, working quickly around the tin in a cartwheel shape.

3 Add the filling and level the surface. Fold in the overhanging pastry to cover the mixture, filling any gaps with leftover pastry. Drizzle with the remaining melted butter, then cook for 45 minutes until golden.

Serves 10	EASY		NUTRITIONAL INFORMATION	
	Preparation Time 40 minutes, plus cooling	**Cooking Time** 45 minutes	**Per Serving** 311 calories, 15g fat (of which 9g saturates), 33g carbohydrate, 1.7g salt	Vegetarian

Freezing Tip

To freeze Complete the recipe to the end of step 2, put the parcels in a freezerproof container and freeze for up to one month.
To use Put the frozen parcels on a lightly greased baking sheet and complete the recipe.

Chestnut and Butternut Filo Parcels

½ tbsp olive oil

75g (3oz) butter

½ onion, finely chopped

5 fresh rosemary sprigs

½ small butternut squash, peeled and finely chopped

1 celery stalk, finely chopped

½ firm pear, finely chopped

100g (3½oz) peeled, cooked (or vacuum-packed) chestnuts, roughly chopped

1 slice walnut bread, about 50g (2oz), cut into small cubes

8 sheets filo pastry, about 30.5 x 20.5cm (12 x 8in) each

50g (2oz) cream cheese

salt and ground black pepper

1 Heat the oil and 15g (½oz) butter in a medium pan, add the onion and fry gently for 10 minutes. Finely chop one rosemary sprig and add to the pan, along with the squash. Continue to cook for 5 minutes or until everything is soft and golden. Add the celery and pear, and cook for 1–2 minutes. Add the chestnuts, season and mix well. Add the bread to the pan, mix everything together, then set aside to cool.

2 Preheat the oven to 200°C (180°C fan oven) mark 6. Melt the remaining butter in a pan. Brush one sheet of filo pastry with the melted butter and layer another sheet of pastry on top, diagonally. Put a quarter of the chestnut mixture in the centre of the pastry and dot with a quarter of the cream cheese. Brush the edges of the pastry with a little more butter, bring the edges up and over the filling and pinch together tightly to make a parcel. Repeat to make three more parcels.

3 Put the parcels on a lightly greased baking sheet and cook for 25–30 minutes until the pastry is golden and the filling is piping hot; 5 minutes before the end of the cooking time, put a rosemary sprig into the top of each parcel. Serve hot.

EASY		NUTRITIONAL INFORMATION		Serves
Preparation Time 40 minutes	**Cooking Time** 45–50 minutes	**Per Serving** 408 calories, 22g fat (of which 13g saturates), 49g carbohydrate, 0.5g salt	Vegetarian	**4**

Get Ahead

Complete the recipe to the end of step 4, then cover and chill overnight until ready to cook.

Wild Mushroom Pithiviers

450g (1lb) wild mushrooms
300ml ($\frac{1}{2}$ pint) milk
200ml (7fl oz) double cream
2 garlic cloves, crushed
450g (1lb) floury potatoes, peeled and thinly sliced
freshly grated nutmeg
50g (2oz) butter
2 tsp freshly chopped thyme, plus fresh sprigs to garnish
2 x 500g packs puff pastry, thawed if frozen
flour to dust
1 large egg, beaten
salt and ground black pepper

1 Rinse the mushrooms in cold running water to remove any grit, then pat dry with kitchen paper. Roughly slice.

2 Put the milk and cream in a large heavy-based pan with the crushed garlic. Bring to the boil, then add the potatoes. Bring back to the boil and simmer gently, stirring occasionally, for 15–20 minutes until the potatoes are tender. Season with salt, pepper and nutmeg. Leave to cool.

3 Melt the butter in a large frying pan. When it's sizzling, add the mushrooms and cook over a high heat, stirring all the time, for 5–10 minutes until the mushrooms are cooked and the juices have evaporated completely. Season. Stir in the chopped thyme, then set aside to cool.

4 On a lightly floured surface, roll out the pastry thinly. Cut into eight rounds, approximately 12.5cm (5in) in diameter, for the tops and eight rounds, approximately 11.5cm (4$\frac{1}{2}$in) in diameter, for the bases. Put the smaller pastry rounds on baking sheets and brush the edges with beaten egg. Put a large spoonful of the cooled potato mixture in the centre of each round, leaving a 1cm ($\frac{1}{2}$in) border around the edge. Top with a spoonful of the mushroom mixture, then cover with the pastry tops. Press the edges together well to seal. Chill for 30 minutes–1 hour.

5 Meanwhile preheat the oven to 220°C (200°C fan oven) mark 7 and put two baking trays in to heat up. Use the back of a knife to scallop the edges of the pastry and brush the top with the remaining beaten egg. If you like, use a knife to decorate the tops of the pithiviers.

6 Put the pithiviers, on their baking sheets, on the preheated baking trays. Cook for 15–20 minutes until deep golden brown, swapping the trays around in the oven halfway through cooking. Serve immediately, garnished with thyme sprigs.

EASY		NUTRITIONAL INFORMATION		Serves
Preparation Time 1 hour, plus 1 hour chilling and cooling	**Cooking Time** about 1 hour	**Per Serving** 710 calories, 51g fat (of which 12g saturates), 58g carbohydrate, 1.2g salt	Vegetarian	**8**

Freezing Tip

To freeze Complete the recipe to the end of step 2, then wrap and freeze for up to one month.
To use Cook from frozen in a preheated oven at 200°C (180°C fan oven) mark 6 for 25 minutes until the pastry is golden. Complete the recipe.

Leek, Artichoke and Mushroom Croûte

3 tbsp olive oil

2 garlic cloves, crushed

125g (4oz) shiitake mushrooms, sliced

1 tbsp balsamic vinegar

50g (2oz) peeled cooked (or vacuum-packed) chestnuts, roughly chopped

1½ tsp fresh thyme leaves

400g can artichoke hearts, drained and quartered

350g (12oz) leeks, sliced

375g pack ready-rolled puff pastry

butter to grease

1 medium egg, lightly beaten

salt and ground black pepper

cranberry sauce and a little extra virgin olive oil to serve

1   Heat 2 tbsp olive oil in a large pan and fry the garlic for 1 minute. Add the mushrooms and cook over a low heat for 3 minutes to soften. Add the vinegar, chestnuts, ½ tsp thyme leaves and the artichokes, then cook for 1 minute. In a separate pan, soften the leeks in the remaining 1 tbsp oil for 4 minutes. Tip into a bowl and cool for 5 minutes.

2   Unroll the pastry and sprinkle with the remaining thyme; roll it lightly into the pastry. Flip the pastry over so that the herbs are on the underside, then lightly roll out to a 38 x 25.5cm (15 x 10in) rectangle. Using a sharp knife, cut the pastry in half to create two long, thin rectangles. Spoon half the mushroom mixture down the centre of each. Top with the leeks and season. Brush the pastry edges with water, then fold each side of the pastry up over the filling and seal. Cut both rolls in half and put on to a greased baking sheet. Cover and chill overnight.

3   Preheat the oven to 200°C (180°C fan oven) mark 6. Brush the pastry with egg to glaze. Cook for 20 minutes until the pastry is golden. Slice each croûte into six and serve three slices per person, with cranberry sauce and a light drizzle of olive oil.

Serves 8	EASY		NUTRITIONAL INFORMATION	
	Preparation Time 30 minutes, plus cooling and chilling overnight	**Cooking Time** 30–35 minutes	**Per Serving** 236 calories, 17g fat (of which 1g saturates), 20g carbohydrate, 0.4g salt	Vegetarian

125g (4oz) fresh spinach leaves

2 tbsp sunflower oil

1 onion, finely chopped

1 large garlic clove, chopped

250g (9oz) soft goat's cheese

275g (10oz) filo pastry, thawed if frozen

50g (2oz) butter, melted

sesame seeds to sprinkle

salt and ground black pepper

Goat's Cheese Parcels

1 Plunge the spinach into a pan of boiling water, bring back to the boil for 1 minute, then drain and refresh under very cold water. Squeeze out all the excess liquid and chop finely.

2 Heat the oil in a pan, add the onion and garlic, and cook until translucent, then allow to cool. Combine the spinach, onion mixture and goat's cheese in a bowl, and season generously.

3 Cut the pastry into twenty-four 12.5cm (5in) squares. Brush one square with melted butter, cover with a second square and brush with more butter. Put to one side and cover with a damp teatowel. Repeat with the remaining squares, to make twelve sets.

4 Put a dessertspoonful of the filling on each square and join up the corners to form a parcel. Brush with a little more butter, sprinkle with sesame seeds and chill for 20 minutes. Meanwhile, preheat the oven to 220°C (200°C fan oven) mark 7. Bake for about 5 minutes or until the pastry is crisp and browned.

EASY		NUTRITIONAL INFORMATION		Serves
Preparation Time 45 minutes, plus 10 minutes cooling	**Cooking Time** 10 minutes	**Per Serving (2 parcels per serving)** 345 calories, 22g fat (of which 12g saturates), 26g carbohydrate, 0.8g salt	Vegetarian	**6**

Cook's Tip

Home-made pesto: whiz 2 roughly chopped garlic cloves in a mini food processor with a pinch of salt, 40g (1½oz) pinenuts, 20g (¾oz) basil leaves, 2 tbsp olive oil and 15g (½oz) freshly grated Parmesan. Alternatively, to make in a pestle and mortar, pound the garlic to a paste with a little salt, then add the pinenuts and basil, and continue pounding until smooth. Work in the grated Parmesan, then gradually beat in the oil.

Salmon with Pesto en Croûte

¼ filleted whole salmon, about 450g (1lb), skinned and boned

pesto (see Cook's Tip)

75g (3oz) Parma ham, thinly sliced

375g pack ready-rolled puff pastry

flour to dust

1 medium egg, lightly beaten

salt and ground black pepper

1 Spread the salmon with the pesto and wrap in Parma ham. Wrap in clingfilm and chill for 30 minutes.

2 Preheat the oven to 220°C (200°C fan oven) mark 7. Cut one-third off the end of the pastry, then roll out the smaller piece on a lightly floured surface to 3mm (⅛in) thick and 1cm (½in) larger than the salmon all round. Prick with a fork, transfer to a baking sheet, then cook for 10–12 minutes until golden and crisp.

3 Leave until cool, then put the salmon on top. Reduce the oven temperature to 200°C (180°C fan oven) mark 6. Unroll the remaining pastry on a lightly floured surface. Dust a lattice cutter with flour, then roll firmly over the pastry. Gently ease each lattice open with a sharp knife. Alternatively, make a lattice effect with a small sharp knife. Cover the salmon with lattice pastry and tuck the ends underneath. Seal the edges and trim off any excess. Brush with beaten egg. Cook on a foil-lined baking sheet for 30–35 minutes until the pastry is crisp and golden. Serve warm.

	EASY		NUTRITIONAL INFORMATION
Serves 6	**Preparation Time** 25–30 minutes, plus 30 minutes chilling	**Cooking Time** about 45 minutes	**Per Serving** 495 calories, 35g fat (of which 3g saturates), 24g carbohydrate, 1.1g salt

Salmon, Dill and Potato Pastries

1 potato, about 125g (4oz), peeled and cut into 5mm (¼in) cubes

300ml (½ pint) single cream

2 tbsp freshly chopped dill

250g (9oz) skinned salmon fillet, cut into 5mm (¼in) cubes

flour to dust

700g (1½lb) puff pastry, thawed if frozen

1 medium egg, beaten

salt and ground black pepper

1 Put the potato in a pan with the cream, bring to the boil and simmer gently for 5 minutes or until the potato is almost tender. Cool, then add the dill and salmon, and season well.

2 Roll out the pastry on a lightly floured surface to 3mm (⅛in) thick, then stamp out twelve rounds 7.5cm (3in) in diameter and twelve rounds 9.5cm (3¾in) in diameter.

3 Put the smaller rounds on a baking sheet, brush the edges with cold water and spoon about 2 tbsp of the salmon mixture into the centre. Top with the larger rounds, seal and crimp the edges, then cut a steam hole in the centre. Chill for 10 minutes.

4 Put a baking tray in the oven and preheat to 220°C (200°C fan oven) mark 7. Brush the pastries with the beaten egg and put the baking sheet on to the hot baking tray. Cook for 20 minutes or until the pastry is crisp and brown. Serve warm.

EASY		NUTRITIONAL INFORMATION	Serves
Preparation Time 40 minutes, plus 20 minutes cooling	**Cooking Time** 25 minutes	**Per Serving (2 pastries per serving)** 345 calories, 22g fat (of which 12g saturates), 26g carbohydrate, 1.8g salt	**6**

275g (10oz) plain flour, plus extra to dust

200g (7oz) chilled butter, cubed

a pinch of salt

1 large egg, beaten, plus 1 large egg, beaten, to glaze

For the filling

2 large eggs and 2 large yolks, beaten

200ml (7fl oz) crème fraîche

3 tbsp freshly chopped dill

450g (1lb) fresh salmon fillet, cut into wide strips, 10cm (4in) long

200g (7oz) button mushrooms, sliced and fried in 25g (1oz) butter for 1–2 minutes, cooled

150g (5oz) thick asparagus tips, blanched, drained and refreshed in iced water

salt and ground black pepper

Cook's Tips

To check the pie is cooked, insert a skewer in the centre for 30 seconds – it should feel hot when you pull it out. **Cool the pie** in the tin for 1 hour to serve warm, or 3 hours to serve at room temperature.

Salmon and Asparagus Pie

1 Whiz the flour, butter and salt in a food processor until the mixture resemble breadcrumbs. Add one egg and 2 tbsp cold water and pulse until the mixture just comes together. Knead lightly on a floured surface. Cut off one-third, wrap both pieces and chill for 30 minutes. Preheat the oven to 200°C (180°C fan oven) mark 6. Roll out the larger piece to a 28cm (11in) round and line a 20.5cm (8in) loose-based deep tin. Bake blind (see page 16) for 25 minutes. Remove the paper and beans, brush the pastry with beaten egg and cook for 5–10 minutes. Cool.

2 To make the filling, mix the eggs and yolks, crème fraîche and dill; season. Put half the fish in the pie case, arrange the vegetables on top and season. Finish with fish and pour over the crème fraîche mixture to within 1cm (½in) of the top. Brush the rim with beaten egg. Cut the remaining pastry into a 25.5cm (10in) round, place on top and seal the edges. Brush with egg. Make a steam hole. Put a baking tray in the oven. Bake the pie on the hot tray for 40 minutes or until golden and the filling is cooked.

Serves 6	EASY		NUTRITIONAL INFORMATION
	Preparation Time 40 minutes, plus 1½ hours chilling and cooling	**Cooking Time** 1 hour 10 minutes	**Per Serving** 782 calories, 59g fat (of which 32g saturates), 37g carbohydrate, 0.8g salt

Try Something Different

For a vegetarian alternative, replace the chicken with 200g (7oz) cooked, peeled (or vacuum-packed) chestnuts, roughly chopped. Add another leek and increase the quantity of mushrooms to 300g (11oz).

Chicken and Mushroom Pies

2 tbsp olive oil

1 leek, about 200g (7oz), finely sliced

2–3 garlic cloves, crushed

350g (12oz) boneless, skinless chicken thighs, cut into 2.5cm (1in) cubes

200g (7oz) chestnut mushrooms, sliced

150ml (¼ pint) double cream

2 tbsp freshly chopped thyme

500g pack puff pastry, thawed if frozen

flour to dust

1 medium egg, beaten

salt and ground black pepper

1. Heat the oil in a pan and fry the leek over a medium heat for 5 minutes. Add the garlic and cook for 1 minute. Add the chicken and continue to cook for 8–10 minutes. Add the mushrooms and cook for 5 minutes or until all the juices have disappeared.

2. Pour the cream into the pan and bring to the boil. Cook for 5 minutes to make a thick sauce. Add the thyme, then season well with salt and pepper. Tip into a bowl and leave to cool.

3. Roll out the pastry on a lightly floured surface until it measures 33 x 33cm (13 x 13in). Cut into four squares. Brush the edges with water and spoon the chicken mixture into the middle of each square. Bring each corner of the square up to the middle to make a parcel. Crimp the edges to seal, leaving a small hole in the middle. Brush the pies with beaten egg, put on a baking sheet and chill for 20 minutes.

4. Preheat the oven to 200°C (180°C fan oven) mark 6. Cook the pies for 30–40 minutes until golden.

EASY		NUTRITIONAL INFORMATION	Serves
Preparation Time 20 minutes, plus 20 minutes chilling	**Cooking Time** 55 minutes–1 hour 5 minutes	**Per Serving** 805 calories, 58g fat (of which 14g saturates), 49g carbohydrate, 1.2g salt	**4**

Try Something Different

Replace the artichoke hearts with 225g (8oz) brown-cap mushrooms, cooked in a little water with seasoning and lemon juice.

Chicken and Artichoke Pie

3 boneless, skinless chicken breasts, about 350g (12oz)

150ml (¼ pint) dry white wine

225g (8oz) reduced-fat soft cheese with garlic and herbs

400g can artichoke hearts, drained and quartered

4 sheets filo pastry, thawed if frozen

olive oil

1 tsp sesame seeds

salt and ground black pepper

1 Preheat the oven to 200°C (180°C fan oven) mark 6. Put the chicken and wine in a pan and bring to the boil, then cover and simmer for 10 minutes. Remove the chicken with a slotted spoon and set aside. Add the cheese to the wine and mix until smooth. Bring to the boil, then simmer the sauce until thickened.

2 Cut the chicken into bite-size pieces, then add to the sauce with the artichokes. Season and mix well.

3 Put the mixture in an ovenproof dish. Brush the pastry lightly with oil, scrunch slightly and put on top of the chicken. Sprinkle with sesame seeds, then cook for 30–35 minutes until crisp. Serve hot.

Serves 4	EASY		NUTRITIONAL INFORMATION
	Preparation Time 20 minutes	**Cooking Time** 45 minutes	**Per Serving** 241 calories, 9g fat (of which 5g saturates), 7g carbohydrate, 0.2g salt

Try Something Different

Replace the chicken with 450g (1lb) cooked turkey meat and replace the tarragon with chopped fresh thyme leaves.

Easy Chicken and Ham Pie

4 ready-roasted chicken breasts, shredded
100g (3½oz) cooked smoked ham, cubed
150ml (¼ pint) double cream
75ml (2½fl oz) chicken gravy
2 tbsp finely chopped tarragon
1 tsp cornflour
½ tsp English mustard
250g (9oz) ready-rolled puff pastry
1 medium egg, beaten
ground black pepper

1 Preheat the oven to 200°C (180°C fan oven) mark 6. Put the chicken in a large bowl with the ham, then add the cream, gravy, tarragon, cornflour and mustard. Season with black pepper and mix well.

2 Spoon into a shallow 1 litre (1¾ pint) baking dish. Unroll the puff pastry and position over the top of the dish to cover. Trim to fit the dish, then press the edges down lightly around the rim. Brush the egg over the pastry. Cook for 30–35 minutes until the pastry is golden and puffed up. Serve hot.

EASY		NUTRITIONAL INFORMATION	Serves
Preparation Time 15 minutes	**Cooking Time** 30–35 minutes	**Per Serving** 364 calories, 22g fat (of which 6g saturates), 17g carbohydrate, 1.1g salt	**6**

Freezing Tip

To freeze Cover the uncooked galette in clingfilm and freeze on the baking sheet. When firm, remove from the baking tray. Wrap in baking parchment, and then in clingfilm.

To use Thaw for 3 hours at cool room temperature on baking parchment. Preheat the oven to 220°C (200°C fan oven) mark 7 and put a baking tray in the oven to heat. Brush the galette with beaten egg and sprinkle with cheese. Put the galette on the hot tray (this will keep the pastry base crisp) and bake for 40 minutes.

Leek and Ham Galette

25g (1oz) butter, plus extra to grease
350g (12oz) medium leeks, trimmed and cut into 2cm (³⁄₄in) thick slices
25g (1oz) plain flour, plus extra to dust
50ml (2fl oz) milk
1 tbsp freshly chopped marjoram
50g (2oz) Gruyère cheese, cubed, plus 2 tbsp, grated
150g (5oz) cooked sliced ham, thickly shredded
225g (8oz) puff pastry, thawed if frozen
¹⁄₂ medium egg, beaten with a pinch of salt
salt and ground black pepper

1 Preheat the oven to 220°C (200°C fan oven) mark 7. Grease a baking sheet. Cook the leeks in boiling salted water for 2–3 minutes until just beginning to soften. Drain, keeping the cooking liquid to one side. Plunge the leeks into cold water, drain and dry well on kitchen paper.

2 Melt the butter in a pan, remove from the heat and mix in the flour to form a smooth paste. Mix in 225ml (8fl oz) leek water and the milk, stirring until smooth. Bring to the boil, simmer for 1–2 minutes, cover and cool for 20 minutes or until cold. Add the marjoram, leeks, cubed cheese and ham, and season.

3 Roll out the pastry on a lightly floured surface to a 30.5 x 33cm (12 x 13in) rectangle. Cut into two rectangles, one 15 x 30.5cm (6 x 12in) and the other 18 x 30.5cm (7 x 12in). Put the smaller piece on to the baking sheet. Spoon on the ham mixture, leaving a 2cm (³⁄₄in) border all the way around. Brush the border with beaten egg. Cover the filling with the larger pastry rectangle and press the edges together. Cut slashes in the top of the pastry to prevent the filling seeping out. Crimp the edges to seal, then cover and freeze for 20 minutes or until firm. Remove from the freezer, brush again with the beaten egg and sprinkle with the grated cheese. Bake for 20–30 minutes until brown and crisp. Serve hot.

Serves	EASY		NUTRITIONAL INFORMATION
4	**Preparation Time** 30 minutes, plus 20 minutes cooling	**Cooking Time** 40 minutes	**Per Serving** 395 calories, 25g fat (of which 6g saturates), 29g carbohydrate, 2g salt

Try Something Different

Add 1 hot red chilli, deseeded and finely chopped, 1 tbsp freshly grated ginger and a handful of chopped fresh coriander leaves to the pork sausagemeat.

450g (1lb) puff pastry, thawed if frozen

450g (1lb) pork sausagemeat

flour to dust

milk to brush

beaten egg to glaze

Sausage Rolls

1 Preheat the oven to 220°C (200°C fan oven) mark 7. Roll out half of the puff pastry on a lightly floured surface to a 40.5 x 20.5cm (16 x 8in) rectangle; cut lengthways into two strips.

2 Divide the sausagemeat into four, dust with flour and form two portions into rolls, the length of the pastry. Lay a sausagemeat roll on each strip of pastry. Brush the pastry edges with a little milk, fold one side of the pastry over and press the long edges together to seal. Repeat with the remaining pastry and sausage meat. Trim the ends.

3 Brush the pastry with egg to glaze and cut each roll into 5cm (2in) lengths. Make two or three slits in the top of each one.

4 Transfer to a baking sheet and cook for 15 minutes. Reduce the oven temperature to 180°C (160°C fan oven) mark 4 and cook for a further 15 minutes. Transfer to a wire rack. Serve hot or cold.

EASY		NUTRITIONAL INFORMATION	Makes
Preparation Time 25 minutes	**Cooking Time** 30 minutes	**Per Sausage Roll** 119 calories, 9g fat (of which 2g saturates), 8g carbohydrate, 0.4g salt	**28**

Steak and Kidney Pie

700g (1½lb) stewing steak, cubed and seasoned

2 tbsp plain flour, plus extra to dust

3 tbsp vegetable oil

25g (1oz) butter

1 small onion, finely chopped

175g (6oz) ox kidney, cut into small pieces

150g (5oz) flat mushrooms, cut into large chunks

small pinch of cayenne pepper

1 tsp anchovy essence

350g (12oz) puff pastry, thawed if frozen

1 large egg, beaten with a pinch of salt, to glaze

salt and ground black pepper

1 Preheat the oven to 170°C (150°C fan oven) mark 3. Toss half the steak with half the flour. Heat the oil in a flameproof, non-stick casserole and add the butter. Fry the steak in batches until brown, remove and put to one side. Repeat with the remaining steak.

2 Add the onion and cook gently until soft. Return the steak to the casserole with 200ml (7fl oz) water, the kidney, mushrooms, cayenne and anchovy essence. Bring to the boil, cover and simmer for 5 minutes.

3 Transfer to the oven and cook for 1 hour or until tender. The sauce should be syrupy. If not, transfer the casserole to the hob, remove the lid, bring to the boil and bubble for 5 minutes to reduce the liquid. Leave the steak mixture to cool.

4 Preheat the oven to 200°C (180°C fan oven) mark 6. Put the steak and kidney mixture into a 900ml (1½ pint) pie dish. Pile it high to support the pastry.

5 Roll out the pastry on a lightly floured surface to 5mm (¼in) thick. Cut off four to six strips, 1cm (½in) wide. Dampen the edge of the dish with cold water, then press the pastry strips on to the edge. Dampen the pastry rim and lay the sheet of pastry on top. Press the surfaces together, trim the edge and press down with the back of a knife to seal. Brush the pastry with the glaze and score with the back of a knife. Put the pie dish on a baking sheet and cook for 30 minutes or until the pastry is golden brown and the filling is hot to the centre.

Freezing Tip

To freeze Complete the recipe but do not glaze or bake. Wrap the uncooked pie and freeze.
To use Thaw at cool room temperature overnight. Glaze the pastry and add 5–10 minutes to the cooking time, covering the pie with foil if the top starts to turn too brown.

Serves 6	EASY		NUTRITIONAL INFORMATION
	Preparation Time 40 minutes, plus cooling	**Cooking Time** about 1½ hours	**Per Serving** 565 calories, 36g fat (of which 8g saturates), 26g carbohydrate, 0.9g salt

Cook's Tips

Instead of mixed game, use boneless chicken.
To make one large pie, use a 23cm (9in) base diameter, 5cm (2in) deep, fluted flan tin. Bake the pastry case blind for 40 minutes, then remove the paper and beans and bake for a further 5–10 minutes.

Game and Herb Pies

900g (2lb) puff pastry, thawed if frozen

beaten egg to seal

700g (1½lb) boneless mixed game, such as rabbit and pheasant, cut into bite-size pieces

1 tbsp dried green peppercorns, crushed

25g (1oz) plain flour

2 tbsp oil

75g (3oz) butter

175g (6oz) rindless, smoked, streaky bacon, cut in one piece, if possible, and roughly chopped

225g (8oz) shallots or button onions, halved if large

4 garlic cloves, crushed

600ml (1 pint) dry white wine

1 tsp dried thyme or 1 tbsp freshly chopped thyme

450ml (¾ pint) double cream

225g (8oz) brown-cap mushrooms, halved or sliced

700g (1½lb) fresh spinach leaves

2 tbsp each freshly chopped basil, parsley, mint and tarragon or 1 tsp dried tarragon

salt and ground black pepper

fresh herb sprigs, garlic slices and green peppercorns in brine, fried in hot oil for 2–3 seconds, then drained on kitchen paper, to garnish

1 Preheat the oven to 200°C (180°C fan oven) mark 6. Roll out the pastry to 3mm (⅛in) thick and use it to line eight 7.5cm (3in) (base-measurement) brioche moulds. Prick the bases. Chill for 10 minutes then bake blind (see page 16) until light golden and crisp.

2 Season the game with crushed peppercorns and roll in flour. In a large flameproof casserole, heat the oil with 50g (2oz) butter. Add the game and bacon in batches and fry for 1–2 minutes until golden. Remove and set aside. Add the shallots or onions to the casserole with the garlic and fry for 3–4 minutes until golden brown. Pour in the wine and dried thyme, if using. Bring to the boil, then bubble for 10 minutes or until reduced and syrupy.

3 Return the game and bacon to the casserole. Season and bring to the boil, then add the cream and fresh thyme, if using, and simmer for a further 8–10 minutes until the liquid is reduced by half. Cover and simmer gently for 20 minutes or until very tender.

4 Heat the remaining butter in a wide-based pan, fry the mushrooms over a high heat until golden, then set aside. In the same pan, cook the spinach for 2–3 minutes until just wilted. Drain and squeeze out all the liquid. Roughly chop and season well. Divide the spinach among the pastry cases. Add the herbs and mushrooms to the game mixture and spoon into the cases. Cover loosely with foil and cook at 180°C (160°C fan oven) mark 4 for 10–15 minutes until piping hot to the centre. Garnish and serve hot.

A LITTLE EFFORT		NUTRITIONAL INFORMATION	Serves
Preparation Time 40 minutes, plus 10 minutes chilling	**Cooking Time** 1 hour	**Per Serving** 1058 calories, 78g fat (of which 27g saturates), 49g carbohydrate, 2.2g salt	**8**

Meat, Fish and Vegetable Tarts

Camembert and Tomato Tarts

½ 375g pack ready-rolled puff pastry

2 tbsp tapenade (see Cook's Tip)

200g (7oz) cherry tomatoes, halved

75g (3oz) Camembert, sliced

1 Preheat the oven to 220°C (200°C fan oven) mark 7. Cut the puff pastry into four pieces. Put on to a baking sheet and cook for 8–10 minutes until risen.

2 Press down the centre of each tart slightly with the back of a fish slice, then spread with the tapenade. Top with the tomatoes and sliced Camembert. Put back into the oven for a further 7–8 minutes until golden brown.

Serves 4	EASY		NUTRITIONAL INFORMATION
	Preparation Time 10 minutes	**Cooking Time** 15–20 minutes	**Per Serving** 253 calories, 17g fat (of which 4g saturates), 19g carbohydrate, 1.1g salt

Try Something Different

Add 200g (7oz) cooked and diced smoked ham to the cheese fondue mixture in step 2, along with the dill.

buter to grease

flour to dust

425g pack puff pastry, thawed if frozen

200g (7oz) each Jarlsberg and Gouda cheese, grated

1 garlic clove, crushed

150ml (¼ pint) single cream

juice of 1 small lemon

½ tsp paprika

2 tsp cornflour

50ml (2fl oz) vodka

2 tbsp freshly chopped dill, plus extra to garnish

Cheese Fondue Tarts

1 Preheat the oven to 220°C (200°C fan oven) mark 7 and grease a 12-cup bun tin or muffin pan. On a lightly floured surface, roll out the pastry to 3mm (⅛in) thick. Cut out twelve 10cm (4in) rounds and put into the tin. Prick the bases and chill for 10 minutes. Line with greaseproof paper and fill with baking beans. Bake for 15–20 minutes, then remove the paper and beans and bake for 5 minutes or until golden.

2 Meanwhile, put the cheese, garlic, cream, lemon juice and paprika in a pan, heat and stir to make a smooth sauce. Mix the cornflour and vodka together, add to the pan and cook for 1–2 minutes. Stir in the dill.

3 Spoon the mixture into the pastry cases, scatter with dill and serve warm.

EASY		NUTRITIONAL INFORMATION		Serves
Preparation Time 20 minutes, plus 10 minutes chilling	**Cooking Time** 25 minutes	**Per Serving (2 tarts per serving)** 337 calories, 22g fat (of which 3g saturates), 28g carbohydrate, 0.6g salt	Vegetarian	**6**

Cook's Tip

The same mixture can be cooked in a 23cm (9in) round tin.

Country Tomato and Parmesan Tart

75g (3oz) plain flour

75g (3oz) butter

150g (5oz) vegetarian Parmesan, finely grated

¼ tsp cayenne pepper

4 tbsp sun-dried tomato paste

15g (½oz) fresh breadcrumbs

900g (2lb) tomatoes, preferably plum, thickly sliced

1 tbsp freshly chopped thyme, plus extra sprigs to garnish

salt and ground black pepper

1 Preheat the oven to 180°C (160°C fan oven) mark 4. In a food processor, blend the flour, butter, 75g (3oz) grated Parmesan, ½ tsp salt and the cayenne pepper until the mixture looks like rough breadcrumbs. Set aside one-third of the mixture, cover and chill. Press the remaining crumb mixture into the base of a 20.5cm (8in) square, loose-based flan tin, using the back of a spoon to spread it out to the edges. Chill for 10 minutes. Cook the crumb base for 15–20 minutes until light golden brown. Cool.

2 Spread the tomato paste over the cooled crumb base, then sprinkle with half the breadcrumbs. Layer the tomato slices and thyme on top and sprinkle with the remaining breadcrumbs, the remaining Parmesan and the reserved crumb mixture. Season with salt and black pepper.

3 Cook the tart in the oven for a further 15–20 minutes until golden brown. Allow it to cool slightly, then cut into portions and garnish with fresh thyme.

Serves 4	EASY		NUTRITIONAL INFORMATION	
	Preparation Time 40 minutes, plus chilling	**Cooking Time** 40 minutes	**Per Serving** 274 calories, 19g fat (of which 12g saturates), 37g carbohydrate, 0.9g salt	Vegetarian

Freezing Tip

The baskets can be frozen at the end of step 1.
To use Thaw, then complete the recipe.

Mushroom Baskets

250g (9oz) plain flour, plus extra to dust
150g (5oz) chilled butter, cubed
1 large egg

For the filling

50g (2oz) butter
225g (8oz) onion, finely chopped
450g (1lb) mixed mushrooms, sliced
1 garlic clove, crushed
15g (½oz) dried mushrooms, soaked in 300ml (½ pint) boiling water for 10 minutes
300ml (½ pint) medium-dry sherry
300ml (½ pint) double cream
salt and ground black pepper
fresh thyme sprigs to garnish
green salad to serve

1 Whiz the flour and butter in a food processor until the mixture resembles fine breadcrumbs. Add the egg and pulse until the mixture comes together. Knead lightly on a floured surface and shape into six balls. Wrap and chill for 30 minutes. Roll out the pastry on a lightly floured surface and line six loose-based tart tins 9cm (3½in) across the base. Prick the bases and chill for 20 minutes. Meanwhile, preheat the oven to 200°C (180°C fan oven) mark 6. Bake the pastry bases blind (see page 16). Reduce the oven temperature to 180°C (160°C fan oven) mark 4.

2 To make the filling, heat the butter in a pan, add the onion and cook for 10 minutes. Add the sliced mushrooms and garlic, cook for 5 minutes, remove and set aside. Put the dried mushrooms and their liquid in the pan with the sherry. Bring to the boil, bubble for 10 minutes, add the cream and cook for 5 minutes or until syrupy. To serve, warm the pastry in the oven for 5 minutes. Add the reserved mushrooms to the sauce, season and heat through. Pour into the cases, garnish with thyme and serve with salad.

EASY		NUTRITIONAL INFORMATION		Serves
Preparation Time 40 minutes, plus 50 minutes chilling	**Cooking Time** 50 minutes	**Per Serving** 659 calories, 48g fat (of which 29g saturates), 37g carbohydrate, 0.5g salt	Vegetarian	**6**

Roasted Vegetable and Rocket Tartlets

375g pack ready-rolled puff pastry

flour to dust

1 medium egg, beaten

2 tbsp coarse sea salt

300g (11oz) vegetable antipasti in olive oil (such as mixed roasted peppers, artichokes and onions)

a little olive oil, if needed

2 tbsp balsamic vinegar

190g tub red pepper hummus

50g (2oz) wild rocket

salt and ground black pepper

1 Preheat the oven to 220°C (200°C fan oven) mark 7. Unroll the puff pastry on a lightly floured surface and cut it into six equal-sized squares.

2 Put the pastry squares on a large baking sheet and prick each one all over with a fork. Brush all over with beaten egg and sprinkle the edges with sea salt. Cook for 5–7 minutes until the pastry is golden brown and cooked through.

3 Pour off 4 tbsp olive oil from the antipasti into a bowl (top it up with a little more olive oil if there's not enough in the antipasti jar). Add the balsamic vinegar. Season well with salt and pepper, mix well, then set aside.

4 To serve, divide the hummus among the pastry bases, spreading it over each. Put the bases on individual plates and spoon over the antipasti – there's no need to be neat.

5 Whisk the balsamic vinegar dressing together. Add the rocket leaves and toss to coat, then pile a small handful of leaves on top of each tartlet.

Get Ahead

Make the tartlets to the end of step 2. Cool on a wire rack, then store in an airtight container for up to two days. **To use** Complete the recipe.

Serves	EASY		NUTRITIONAL INFORMATION	
6	**Preparation Time** 15 minutes	**Cooking Time** 5–7 minutes	**Per Serving** 371 calories, 26g fat (of which 1g saturates), 30g carbohydrate, 1.1g salt	Vegetarian

Cook's Tip

Cranberry and Red Onion Marmalade: heat 2 tbsp olive oil in a pan and gently fry 500g (1lb 2oz) sliced red onions for 5 minutes. Add the juice of 1 orange, 1 tbsp pickling spice, 150g (5oz) dark muscovado sugar and 150ml (¼ pint) ruby port, and simmer gently for 40 minutes. Add 450g (1lb) fresh cranberries and cook over a medium heat for 20 minutes. Cool and chill for up to two days.

Winter Roasted Vegetable Tart

250g pack ready-rolled shortcrust pastry, removed from refrigerator 5 minutes before using

1 small red onion, cut into six wedges

1 raw baby beetroot, peeled and thickly sliced

1 baby aubergine, quartered

1 small red apple, quartered, cored and cut into chunky slices

1 garlic clove, crushed

juice of ½ lemon

1 tsp freshly chopped thyme

1 tbsp olive oil

125g (4oz) Cranberry and Red Onion Marmalade (see Cook's Tip)

25g (1oz) chestnut mushrooms, sliced

50g (2oz) cooked and peeled (or vacuum-packed) chestnuts, chopped

1 tbsp redcurrant jelly, warmed

salt and ground black pepper

1 Preheat the oven to 200°C (180°C fan oven) mark 6. Put an 11.5 x 20.5cm (4½ x 8in) loose-based rectangular tart tin on a baking sheet. Line the tin with the pastry, prick the base and bake blind (see page 16). Cool and remove from the tin.

2 Put the onion, beetroot, aubergine, apple and garlic into a roasting tin. Squeeze over the lemon juice, scatter over the thyme and drizzle with oil, then roast for 20 minutes. Tip into a bowl, then cool.

3 Put the cooked pastry case on a baking sheet. Spoon the Cranberry and Red Onion Marmalade over the base. Arrange the roasted vegetables and mushrooms on top of the tart. Sprinkle the chestnuts on top, then season. Brush warmed redcurrant jelly over the vegetables and cook for 20 minutes. Serve hot.

	EASY		NUTRITIONAL INFORMATION	
Serves **6**	**Preparation Time** marmalade, 10 minutes tart, 20 minutes	**Cooking Time** marmalade, about 1 hour tart, 1 hour	**Per Serving** 540 calories, 24g fat (of which 1g saturates), 85g carbohydrate, 0.5g salt	Vegetarian

Get Ahead

To prepare ahead Cook the onions as in step 1, cover and chill for up to one day.
To use Complete the recipe.

Pissaladière

4 tbsp olive oil
3 large Spanish onions, very finely sliced
1 garlic clove, crushed
375g pack ready-rolled puff pastry
125g (4oz) roasted red peppers in oil, drained and cut into thin strips
50g can anchovies in olive oil, drained
12 black pitted olives, halved
1 tsp mixed dried herbs
salt and ground black pepper

1   Preheat the oven to 220°C (200°C fan oven) mark 7. Heat the oil in a deep frying pan and stir in the onions and garlic. Season with salt and pepper. Cook, uncovered, over a gentle heat for 30–40 minutes, stirring occasionally to make sure the vegetables don't stick, until the onions are meltingly soft and pale golden.

2   While the onions are cooking, unroll the pastry, cut into six equal rectangles, then arrange on two small baking sheets.

3   Divide the cooked onion among the pastry bases and spread out evenly, leaving a 1cm (½in) gap around the edges. Arrange the red pepper in a diamond-shaped lattice pattern over the onions.

4   Cut the anchovies in half lengthways and arrange on top of the onions. Dot the olives over the top. Sprinkle over the dried herbs, then cook for 20–25 minutes until the pastry is golden and crisp.

EASY		NUTRITIONAL INFORMATION	Serves
Preparation Time 10 minutes	**Cooking Time** 1 hour 5 minutes	**Per Serving** 411 calories, 28g fat (of which 2g saturates), 3.5g carbohydrate, 1.8g salt	**6**

Soured Cream and Onion Tarts

700g (1½lb) tomatoes, halved

1 tbsp freshly chopped thyme or 1 tsp dried

2 tbsp olive oil

200g (7oz) chilled butter

175g (6oz) plain flour, plus extra to dust

6–7 tbsp soured cream

900g (2lb) onions, finely sliced

125g (4oz) Roquefort cheese

salt and ground black pepper

1 Preheat the oven to 170°C (150°C fan oven) mark 3. Put the tomatoes on a baking sheet. Season and sprinkle with thyme, drizzle with oil and cook, uncovered, for 40 minutes until slightly shrivelled. Leave to cool.

2 Meanwhile, cut 150g (5oz) of the butter into small dice and put in a food processor with the flour. Pulse until the butter is roughly cut up through the flour (you should still be able to see pieces of butter), then add the soured cream and pulse again for 2–3 seconds until just mixed. (Alternatively, rub the fat into the flour in a large bowl by hand or using a pastry cutter. Stir in the cream using a fork.)

3 On a lightly floured surface, cut the pastry into six and thinly roll each into a 12.5cm (5in) round. Put on two baking sheets, cover and chill for 30 minutes.

4 Meanwhile, melt the remaining butter in a pan, add the onions and cook over a low heat for 15 minutes until very soft. Increase the heat for 3–4 minutes until the onions are well browned. Cool.

5 Spoon the onions into the centre of the pastries, leaving a 1cm (½in) edge. Crumble the cheese on top and add the tomatoes. Season, then roughly fold up the pastry edge. Chill for 20 minutes. Preheat the oven to 200°C (180°C fan oven) mark 6. Cook the tarts for 30 minutes until golden. Serve immediately.

Try Something Different

Other cheeses to try with this pie are feta, crumbly goat's cheese, Red Leicester or other blue cheese.

Omit the tomatoes and fry 150g (5oz) diced chorizo along with the onions for the final 3–4 minutes in step 4. Top the tarts with strips of roasted red pepper (from a jar) in step 5, then bake.

EASY		NUTRITIONAL INFORMATION		Serves
Preparation Time 20 minutes, plus 50 minutes chilling	**Cooking Time** 1½ hours, plus cooling	**Per Serving** 556 calories, 41g fat (of which 24g saturates), 39g carbohydrate, 1.2g salt	Vegetarian	**6**

Cook's Tip

Using vegetarian Parmesan makes this tart suitable for vegetarians, as traditional Parmesan contains calves' rennet.

Caramelised Onion and Goat's Cheese Tart

230g ready-made shortcrust pastry case

275g jar onion confit

300g (11oz) mild soft goat's cheese

1 medium egg, beaten

25g (1oz) freshly grated vegetarian Parmesan

50g (2oz) wild rocket

balsamic vinegar and extra virgin olive oil to drizzle

salt and ground black pepper

1 Preheat the oven to 200°C (180°C fan oven) mark 6. Line the pastry case with greaseproof paper, fill with baking beans and bake blind (see page 16) for 10 minutes. Remove the paper and beans, prick the pastry base all over with a fork and cook for a further 15–20 minutes until golden.

2 Spoon the onion confit into the pastry case. Beat the goat's cheese and egg together in a bowl until smooth, season with salt and pepper, then spoon on top of the onions. Level the surface with a knife, and sprinkle over the Parmesan. Cook the tart for 25–30 minutes until the filling is set and just beginning to turn golden.

3 Leave to cool for 15 minutes, then cut away the sides of the foil case and carefully slide the tart on to a plate. Just before serving, arrange the rocket on top of the tart and drizzle with balsamic vinegar and olive oil. Serve warm.

Serves 6	EASY		NUTRITIONAL INFORMATION	
	Preparation Time 10 minutes	**Cooking Time** 1 hour	**Per Serving** 480 calories, 28g fat (of which 14g saturates), 44g carbohydrate, 1.5g salt	Vegetarian

Cook's Tips

Orange Vinaigrette: put the zest of 1 orange and 4 tbsp orange juice in a small bowl with ½ tsp Dijon mustard and 2 tsp white wine vinegar. Season with salt and pepper. Whisk until combined, then whisk in 6 tbsp olive oil.
Instead of lobster, use 300g (11oz) cooked peeled large prawns.

Lobster and Summer Vegetable Tartlets

200g (7oz) filo pastry, thawed if frozen

25g (1oz) butter, melted

1 tbsp poppy seeds

a large pinch of saffron, soaked in 1tbsp boiling water for 15 minutes

200ml carton crème fraîche

2 x 700g (1½lb) cooked lobsters, split

125g (4oz) green beans

225g (8oz) slim asparagus tips

125g (4oz) broad beans

4 tbsp Orange Vinaigrette (see Cook's Tip)

salt and ground black pepper

lime wedges to serve

1 Preheat the oven to 190°C (170°C fan oven) mark 5. Cut 16 squares of filo pastry, each 18cm (7in). Brush the squares with melted butter and layer four on top of each other to form a star shape. Put four ovenproof saucers upside down on a baking sheet. Brush with melted butter. Sprinkle the filo shapes with poppy seeds and press each star shape on to a saucer. Cook for 7 minutes or until golden. Cool, then ease off the saucers and set aside.

2 Mix the saffron and its soaking liquid into the crème fraîche, season with salt and pepper, cover and chill.

3 Remove the lobster meat from the claws and from the tail. Chill until needed. Cook the green beans in salted boiling water for about 5 minutes until just tender. Drain, then plunge immediately into ice-cold water. Cook the asparagus and broad beans in the same way for 3 minutes. Drain all the vegetables and dry on kitchen paper. Put in a large bowl and toss in the Orange Vinaigrette – use just enough to moisten the vegetables. Season to taste.

4 To serve, divide the vegetables among the pastry cases. Add the lobster meat and a spoonful of the crème fraîche. Serve with lime wedges.

A LITTLE EFFORT		NUTRITIONAL INFORMATION	Serves
Preparation Time 45 minutes	**Cooking Time** about 10 minutes	**Per Serving** 637 calories, 36g fat (of which 19g saturates), 36g carbohydrate, 1.5g salt	**4**

Get Ahead

Complete the recipe to the end of step 4. Cover
the prawns, vegetables and pastry separately and chill
overnight.
To use Complete the recipe.
To freeze Complete the recipe to the end of step 4. Pack
the pastry, prawns and vegetables separately and freeze for
up to one month.
To use Thaw at cool room temperature then complete the
recipe.

30 raw large prawns, shells on, about 400g (14oz) total
weight

4 tbsp olive oil

2 shallots, peeled and finely chopped

2 garlic cloves, peeled and roughly chopped

1 bay leaf

150ml (¼ pint) brandy

150ml (¼ pint) white wine

400g can chopped tomatoes

2 tbsp freshly chopped tarragon

175g (6oz) celeriac, peeled and chopped

125g (4oz) carrots, peeled and chopped

175g (6oz) leeks (white part only), roughly chopped

2 tbsp vegetable oil

150ml (¼ pint) double cream

grated zest of ½ lemon

225g (8oz) puff pastry, thawed if frozen

salt and ground black pepper

fresh tarragon sprigs to garnish

celeriac and carrots, shredded, blanched and dressed with
lemon juice and olive oil to serve

1 Cook the prawns in a pan of salted boiling water for
1 minute until the shells are pink. Plunge into a bowl
of cold water to cool. Remove the heads and shells
and put to one side. Cover and chill the prawns.

Prawn Tartlets

2 Heat the olive oil in a large pan, add the shallots and
cook gently for 5 minutes or until soft. Add the
garlic, bay leaf, and prawn heads and shells. Cook
over a high heat for 1 minute, then add the brandy.
(If you're cooking over gas, take care, as the brandy
may ignite.) Allow the liquid to reduce by half, then
add the wine. Bring to the boil and bubble until
reduced by half, then add the tomatoes and season.
Add 1 tbsp tarragon. Cook over a medium-low heat
for 20 minutes. Put a colander over a large bowl,
pour the contents of the pan into the colander and
push through as much liquid as possible. Put the
liquid to one side and discard the heads and shells.

3 Put the celeriac, carrots and leeks in a food processor
and pulse until finely chopped. Heat the oil in a
frying pan, add the vegetables and cook quickly for
2 minutes (don't allow them to colour). Add the
prawn and tomato liquid and cream, bring to the boil
and bubble for 10–15 minutes until thick. Season and
stir in the remaining tarragon and lemon zest. Cool.

4 Preheat the oven to 200°C (180°C fan oven) mark 6.
Roll out the pastry and line six 4cm (1½in) diameter
(at base) brioche tins. Bake blind (see page 16); cool.

5 Divide the vegetable mixture among the pastry cases
and top each with five prawns. Put back in the oven
for 10–15 minutes until hot to the centre. Season
with pepper, garnish with tarragon and serve with
a salad of finely shredded celeriac and carrots.

Serves 6	A LITTLE EFFORT		NUTRITIONAL INFORMATION
	Preparation Time 50 minutes	**Cooking Time** 1¼–1½ hours, plus cooling	**Per Serving** 489 calories, 34g fat (of which 10g saturates), 21g carbohydrate, 1.4g salt

Freezing Tip

To freeze Cool, wrap and freeze at the end of the recipe, before garnishing.
To use Thaw overnight at cool room temperature. Reheat at 200°C (180°C fan oven) mark 6 for 5–10 minutes until hot; garnish.

Shellfish and Saffron Tarts

350g (12oz) plain flour, plus extra to dust

175g (6oz) butter

75g (3oz) freshly grated Parmesan

3 medium eggs

a pinch of saffron

150ml (¼ pint) double cream

3 tbsp freshly chopped chives

225g (8oz) cooked peeled prawns, roughly chopped, or 225g (8oz) white crabmeat

salt and ground black pepper

fresh chives to garnish

1 To make the pastry, whiz the flour, butter and cheese in a food processor until the mixture resembles fine crumbs. (Alternatively, rub the butter into the flour in a large bowl by hand until it resembles fine crumbs, then stir in the cheese.) Add 2 lightly beaten eggs and 3 tbsp iced water; pulse or stir with a fork until the crumbs come together to form a dough. Wrap in clingfilm and chill for 30 minutes.

2 Roll out the pastry thinly on a lightly floured surface. Stamp out rounds with a 5cm (2in) plain cutter and line 60 mini tartlet tins. Prick the bases and chill for 30 minutes, Meanwhile, preheat the oven to 200°C (180°C fan oven) mark 6. Cook the tartlet bases for 10 minutes or until golden.

3 Whisk together the remaining egg, saffron, cream and chives, and season. Fill each pastry case with some prawns or crabmeat, and top with 1 tsp of the saffron mixture. Cook for 5–10 minutes. Garnish with chives and serve immediately.

Makes 60	EASY		NUTRITIONAL INFORMATION
	Preparation Time 50 minutes, plus 1 hour chilling	**Cooking Time** 20 minutes	**Per Tart** 66 calories, 5g fat (of which 3g saturates), 5g carbohydrate, 0.1g salt

Try Something Different

Replace the streaky bacon with 6 long strips of smoked salmon, and the chopped parsley with dill.

Egg and Bacon Tarts

500g pack shortcrust pastry, thawed if frozen

6 rashers smoked streaky bacon

6 medium eggs

3 tbsp freshly chopped flat-leafed parsley

1 Preheat the oven to 200°C (180°C fan oven) mark 6 and put two baking sheets into the oven to heat up.

2 Divide the pastry into six pieces, then roll out and use to line six 10cm (4in) fluted flan tins. Prick the bases with a fork. Cover with greaseproof paper, fill with baking beans and chill for 10 minutes.

3 Put the tart tins on to the preheated baking sheets and bake blind (see page 16) for 10 minutes. Remove the paper and beans and cook for a further 5 minutes or until the pastry is dry. Remove the cases from the oven and increase the temperature to 220°C (200°C fan oven) mark 7.

4 Put a rasher of raw bacon across the base of each tart. Crack the eggs into a cup one at a time, adding one to each tart. Season and cook for 10 minutes until the egg white has set. Sprinkle with parsley to serve.

EASY		**NUTRITIONAL INFORMATION**	**Serves**
Preparation Time 20 minutes, plus 10 minutes chilling	**Cooking Time** 25 minutes	**Per Serving** 498 calories, 33g fat (of which 10g saturates), 39g carbohydrate, 1.5g salt	**6**

Cook's Tip

Fill the pastry case as full as possible. You may find you have a little mixture left, as flan tins vary in size.

Quiche Lorraine

Shortcrust Pastry (see page 12) made with 200g (7oz) plain flour, a pinch of salt, 100g (3½oz) chilled butter and 1 large egg

For the filling

5 large eggs

225g (8oz) unsmoked streaky bacon, rind removed

40g (1½oz) butter

125g (4oz) shallots, onions or spring onions, finely chopped

400g (14oz) crème fraîche

100g (3½oz) Gruyère cheese, grated

salt and ground black pepper

crispy bacon and fried spring onions to garnish

1 Preheat the oven to 200°C (180°C fan oven) mark 6. Roll out the pastry thinly and use to line a 23cm (9in), 3cm (1¼in) deep, loose-based tart tin. Prick the base and bake blind (see page 16).

2 Meanwhile, lightly whisk the eggs for the filling. Use a little to brush the inside of the pastry case and return it to the oven for 5 minutes to seal any cracks. Reduce the oven temperature to 190°C (170°C fan oven) mark 5.

3 Cut the bacon into 5mm (¼in) strips. Put the bacon in a pan of cold water and bring to the boil. Drain, refresh under cold water and dry on kitchen paper.

4 Melt the butter in a frying pan, add the shallots or onions and cook for 1 minute. Add the bacon and cook, stirring, until brown.

5 Mix the eggs with the crème fraîche and Gruyère cheese, and season. Put the bacon mixture in the pastry case and spoon the crème fraîche mixture on top (see Cook's Tip). Cook for 30–35 minutes until golden and just set. Cool for 10 minutes before serving. Garnish with bacon and fried spring onions.

Serves 8	EASY		NUTRITIONAL INFORMATION
	Preparation Time 35 minutes, plus 30 minutes chilling	**Cooking Time** 1 hour	**Per Serving** 595 calories, 50g fat (of which 29g saturates), 22g carbohydrate, 1.5g salt

3

Sweet Pies and Pastries

Try Something Different

Replace the plums with pears, toss them in a little lemon juice, and sprinkle with ½ tsp cinnamon instead of the cardamom.

Plum and Cardamom Pie

flour to dust

250g (9oz) ready-rolled sweet shortcrust pastry

900g (2lb) mixed yellow and red plums, halved, stoned and quartered

2–3 green cardamom pods, split open, seeds removed and crushed or chopped

50–75g (2–3oz) caster sugar, plus extra to sprinkle

beaten egg or milk to glaze

1 Heat a flat baking sheet in the oven at 220°C (200°C fan oven) mark 7. On a lightly floured surface, roll the pastry a little thinner into a 30.5cm (12in) circle. Put it on a floured baking sheet, without a lip if possible.

2 Pile the fruit on to the pastry and sprinkle with the cardamom seeds and sugar (if the plums are tart you'll need all of it; less if they are ripe and sweet). Fold in the pastry edges and pleat together.

3 Brush the pastry with beaten egg or milk and sprinkle with sugar. Put on the preheated sheet and bake for 30 minutes until the pastry is golden brown and the plums just tender. The juices will begin to bubble from the pie as it cooks.

4 Leave to cool for 10 minutes, then carefully loosen the pastry around the edges. Cool for another 20 minutes, then transfer very carefully to a serving plate. Sprinkle with a little sugar and serve warm.

Serves	EASY		NUTRITIONAL INFORMATION	
6	**Preparation Time** 15 minutes	**Cooking Time** 30 minutes, plus 30 minutes cooling	**Per Serving** 275 calories, 12g fat (of which 4g saturates), 41g carbohydrate, 0.4g salt	Vegetarian

Rustic Blackberry and Apple Pie

450g (1lb) ready-made shortcrust pastry

flour to dust

500g (1lb 2oz) eating apples, quartered, cored and cut into chunky wedges

300g (11oz) blackberries

75g (3oz) golden caster sugar, plus 1 tbsp to sprinkle

¼ tsp ground cinnamon

juice of 1 small lemon

1 Preheat the oven to 200°C (180°C fan oven) mark 6. Put the apples, blackberries, 75g (3oz) sugar, the cinnamon and lemon juice in a bowl and toss together, making sure the sugar dissolves in the juice.

2 Grease a 25.5cm (10in) enamel or metal pie dish. Using a lightly floured rolling pin, roll out the pastry on a large sheet of baking parchment to a 30.5cm (12in) circle. Lift up the paper, upturn the pastry on to the pie dish and peel away the paper.

3 Put the prepared fruit in the centre of the pie dish and fold the pastry edges up and over the fruit. Sprinkle with the remaining sugar and bake for 40 minutes or until the fruit is tender and the pastry golden.

EASY		NUTRITIONAL INFORMATION		Serves
Preparation Time 25 minutes	**Cooking Time** 40 minutes	**Per Serving** 372 calories, 19g fat (of which 11g saturates), 49g carbohydrate, 0.4g salt	Vegetarian	**6**

Sugar-crusted Fruit Pie

75g (3oz) hazelnuts
350g (12oz) cherries, stoned
75g (3oz) caster sugar, plus 2 tbsp
175g (6oz) plain flour, plus extra to dust
125g (4oz) butter
275g (10oz) cooking apples, peeled, cored and quartered

1 Spread the hazelnuts over a baking sheet. Toast under a hot grill until golden brown, turning them frequently. Put the hazelnuts in a clean teatowel and rub off the skins. Leave to cool.

2 Put the cherries in a bowl with 25g (1oz) caster sugar. Cover and set aside. For the hazelnut pastry, put 50g (2oz) hazelnuts in a food processor with the flour and pulse to a powder. Remove and set aside. In the food processor, whiz the butter with 50g (2oz) sugar. Add the flour mixture and pulse until it forms a dough. Turn out on to a lightly floured surface and knead lightly, then wrap and chill for 30 minutes. If the pastry cracks, just work it together.

3 Preheat the oven to 180°C (160°C fan oven) mark 4. Cut the apples into small chunks and put in a 900ml (1½ pint) oval pie dish. Spoon the cherries on top. On a lightly floured surface, roll out the pastry to about 5mm (¼in) thick. Cut into 1cm (½in) strips. Dampen the edge of the pie dish with a little water and press a few of the strips on to the rim to cover it. Dampen the pastry rim. Put the remaining strips over the cherries to create a lattice pattern.

4 Brush the pastry with water and sprinkle with the extra sugar. Bake for 30–35 minutes until the pastry is golden. Set aside to cool for 15 minutes.

5 Chop the remaining toasted hazelnuts and sprinkle over the tart. Serve warm.

Get Ahead

Complete the recipe to the end of step 4, then cool, wrap and chill for up to three days.
To use Bake at 180°C (160°C fan oven) mark 4 for 20–25 minutes to heat through. Complete the recipe.
To freeze Complete the recipe to the end of step 3, then wrap and freeze.
To use Brush the pastry with egg and sprinkle the extra sugar on top. Bake from frozen at 180°C (160°C fan oven) mark 4 for 40–45 minutes until golden. Complete the recipe.

	EASY		NUTRITIONAL INFORMATION	
Serves 4	**Preparation Time** 30 minutes, plus 30 minutes chilling	**Cooking Time** about 40 minutes	**Per Serving** 673 calories, 38g fat (of which 17g saturates), 79g carbohydrate, 0.5g salt	Vegetarian

Try Something Different

Add the grated zest of 1 orange instead of the cinnamon.

Rhubarb and Cinnamon Pie

175g (6oz) plain flour, plus extra to dust

125g (4oz) butter, plus extra to grease

150g (5oz) golden caster sugar

700g (1½lb) rhubarb, cut into bite-size chunks

2 tbsp cornflour

½ tsp ground cinnamon

a little milk and sugar to glaze

1 Put the flour, butter and 25g (1oz) sugar in a food processor and whiz until the pastry comes together. (Alternatively, rub the butter into the flour in a large bowl by hand until it resembles fine crumbs. Stir in the sugar. Bring together and knead very briefly to form a ball.) If the dough is slightly sticky, roll it in some flour; chill for 20 minutes. Grease a 23cm (9in) round ovenproof dish with sides at least 5cm (2in) deep. Roll out the pastry on a lightly floured surface to a large circle, leaving the edges uneven. It should be large enough to line the dish and to allow the edges of the pastry to drape over the sides.

2 Preheat the oven to 200°C (180°C fan oven) mark 6. Toss the rhubarb in the remaining sugar, cornflour and cinnamon, and spoon into the dish. Bring the pastry edges up and over the fruit, leaving a gap in the centre. Glaze with milk and sprinkle with sugar.

3 Put on a baking sheet and bake for 50 minutes or until the pastry is golden brown and the juice is bubbling up. Serve hot.

Serves 6	EASY		NUTRITIONAL INFORMATION	
	Preparation Time 15 minutes, plus 20 minutes chilling	**Cooking Time** 50 minutes	**Per Serving** 379 calories, 14g fat (of which 11g saturates), 55g carbohydrate, 0.3g salt	Vegetarian

Get Ahead

To prepare ahead Complete the recipe then cool and store in an airtight container for up to two days.
To use Heat the pie at 180°C (160°C fan oven) mark 4 for 15–20 minutes.
To freeze Complete the recipe then cool, wrap and freeze the pie in its tin.
To use Reheat the pie from frozen at 180°C (160°C fan oven) mark 4 for 25 minutes or until warm. Cover with foil if it gets too dark.

Pecan Pie

Sweet Shortcrust Pastry (see page 12) made with 175g (6oz) plain flour, 75g (3oz) chilled butter, 50g (2oz) icing sugar and 1 medium egg

ice cream to serve

For the filling

125g (4oz) butter

4 tbsp clear honey

25g (1oz) caster sugar

75g (3oz) dark soft brown sugar

3 tbsp double cream

grated zest of 1 small lemon

1 tsp vanilla extract

175g (6oz) pecan nuts

1 Roll the pastry into a 30.5cm (12in) diameter circle and use to line a 20.5cm (8in) diameter, 2.5cm (1in) deep, loose-based fluted tart tin. Put the tin on a baking sheet and chill for 20 minutes. Meanwhile, preheat the oven to 200°C (180°C fan oven) mark 6. Line the pastry case with greaseproof paper and baking beans, and bake for 15 minutes. Remove the paper and beans, then return the pastry case to the oven for a further 10 minutes. Reduce the oven temperature to 150°C (130°C fan oven) mark 2.

2 To make the filling, melt the butter with the honey and sugars over a low heat, bring to the boil without stirring and bubble for 2–3 minutes. Remove from the heat, stir in the cream, lemon zest, vanilla extract and nuts, and leave to cool for 15 minutes.

3 Pour the pecan mixture into the pastry case. Bake for 40 minutes or until the mixture begins to bubble in the middle (cover with foil if it gets too dark). Serve warm with ice cream.

EASY		NUTRITIONAL INFORMATION		Serves
Preparation Time 25 minutes, plus 50 minutes chilling	**Cooking Time** 1 hour 10 minutes, plus cooling	**Per Serving** 549 calories, 40g fat (of which 16g saturates), 45g carbohydrate, 0.4g salt	Vegetarian	**8**

Try Something Different

Use lime zest and juice instead of lemon.

Lemon Meringue Pie

Sweet Shortcrust Pastry (see page 12), made with 225g (8oz) plain flour, a pinch of salt, 2 tbsp caster sugar, 150g (5oz) butter, cut into pieces, 1 egg yolk and 3 tbsp cold water

flour to dust

a little beaten egg

For the filling and topping

7 medium eggs, 4 separated, at room temperature

finely grated zest of 3 lemons

175ml (6fl oz) freshly squeezed lemon juice (about 4 lemons), strained

400g can condensed milk

150ml (¼ pint) double cream

225g (8oz) golden icing sugar

1 Roll out the pastry on a lightly floured surface and use to line a 23cm (9in), 4cm (1½in) deep, loose-based fluted tart tin. Prick the base with a fork. Chill for 30 minutes. Meanwhile, preheat the oven to 190°C (170°C fan oven) mark 5.

2 Line the pastry case with greaseproof paper and baking beans, and bake blind for 10 minutes. Remove the beans and paper, and bake for a further 10 minutes or until golden and cooked. Brush the inside with beaten egg and put back in the oven for 1 minute to seal. Increase the oven temperature to 180°C (160°C fan oven) mark 4.

3 To make the filling, put 4 egg yolks in a bowl with the 3 whole eggs. Add the lemon zest and juice and whisk lightly. Mix in the condensed milk and cream.

4 Pour the filling into the pastry case and bake for 30 minutes or until just set in the centre. Set aside to cool while you prepare the meringue. Increase the oven temperature to 200°C (180°C fan oven) mark 6.

5 For the meringue, whisk the egg whites and icing sugar together in a heatproof bowl set over a pan of gently simmering water, using a hand-held electric whisk, for 10 minutes or until shiny and thick. Take off the heat and continue to whisk at low speed for 5–10 minutes until the bowl is cool. Pile the meringue on to the filling and swirl to form peaks. Bake for 5–10 minutes until the meringue is tinged brown. Leave to stand for about 1 hour, then serve.

EASY		NUTRITIONAL INFORMATION		Serves
Preparation Time 30 minutes, plus 1 hour chilling	**Cooking Time** about 1 hour, plus standing	**Per Serving** 692 calories, 36g fat (of which 21g saturates), 83g carbohydrate, 0.6g salt	Vegetarian	**8**

Try Something Different

Replace the chocolate ice cream with ginger ice cream and the digestive biscuits with ginger nut biscuits.

Banana and Chocolate Ice Cream Pie

500ml tub chocolate ice cream
75g (3oz) butter, plus extra to grease
200g (7oz) plain chocolate digestive biscuits
2 large bananas, sliced
juice of ½ lemon
1 king-size Mars Bar, cut into thin slivers and chilled

1 Take the ice cream out of the freezer and let it soften. Grease and baseline a 20.5cm (8in) loose-based fluted flan tin. Put the butter in a small pan and melt over medium heat.

2 Put the biscuits into a food processor and whiz until they resemble coarse breadcrumbs. (Alternatively, put them in a plastic bag and crush with a rolling pin. Transfer to a bowl.) Pour the melted butter into the processor and blend with the biscuits to combine (or stir into the crumbs in the bowl until well combined). Press into the base of the prepared tin.

3 Toss the bananas in the lemon juice and scatter over the base. Upturn the ice cream tub on to the bananas and use a palette knife to spread it evenly, covering the fruit.

4 Scatter the Mars Bar slices over the ice cream and freeze for at least 1 hour before slicing.

Serves	EASY		NUTRITIONAL INFORMATION	
8	**Preparation Time** 15 minutes, plus 1 hour freezing		**Per Serving** 410 calories, 25g fat (of which 15g saturates), 43g carbohydrate, 0.6g salt	Vegetarian

Cook's Tip

Confectioner's Custard: scrape the vanilla seeds from 1 vanilla pod into a pan. Add the pod and 450ml ($^3/_4$ pint) milk, bring to the boil, then set aside for 30 minutes. Remove the vanilla pod. Whisk 4 large egg yolks and 75g (3oz) caster sugar until pale. Mix in 50g (2oz) plain flour. Strain in a quarter of the infused milk, mix, then stir in the remainder. Return to the pan and bring to the boil over a low heat, stirring. Pour into a bowl, cover with clingfilm, cool and chill for 3–4 hours.

550g (1$^1/_4$lb) puff pastry, thawed if frozen

flour to dust

25g (1oz) caster sugar, plus 3 tbsp

50g (2oz) hazelnuts, toasted and chopped

225g (8oz) raspberries

1 tbsp lemon juice

Confectioner's Custard (see Cook's Tip)

300ml ($^1/_2$ pint) double cream

50g (2oz) icing sugar, sifted

Raspberry Millefeuilles

1 Cut the pastry into three and roll each piece on a lightly floured surface into an 18 x 35.5cm (7 x 14in) rectangle. Put each on a baking sheet, prick and chill for 30 minutes. Preheat the oven to 220°C (200°C fan oven) mark 7. Bake for 10 minutes, turn over and cook for another 3 minutes. Sprinkle each sheet with 1 tbsp caster sugar and one-third of the nuts. Return to the oven for 8 minutes until the sugar melts. Cool slightly, then transfer to wire racks to cool.

2 Sprinkle the raspberries with 25g (1oz) caster sugar and the lemon juice. Beat the custard until smooth; whip the cream until thick, then fold into the custard with the raspberries and juices. Cover and chill. Put the icing sugar in a bowl, then stir in 2 tbsp water. Trim each pastry sheet to 15 x 30.5cm (6 x 12in), then drizzle with the icing. Leave for 15 minutes.

3 Spoon half the custard over a sheet of pastry. Put another sheet on top and spoon over the remaining custard. Top with the final sheet and press down lightly. Leave for 30 minutes before slicing.

EASY		NUTRITIONAL INFORMATION		Serves
Preparation Time 40 minutes, plus chilling and standing	**Cooking Time** 40 minutes, plus cooling	**Per Serving** 828 calories, 57g fat (of which 23g saturates), 65g carbohydrate, 1.4g salt	Vegetarian	**8**

Freezing Tip

To freeze Complete the recipe but do not bake. Freeze the unbaked pies in their tins, covered with clingfilm. When frozen, remove from the tins and pack in an airtight container for up to one month.
To use Bake the mince pies from frozen in the bun tins at 190°C (170°C fan oven) mark 5 for 18–20 minutes until golden.

Cranberry and Apple Mince Pies

For the mincemeat
450g (1lb) Bramley apples, cored and chopped
225g (8oz) fresh cranberries, plus extra to decorate
125g (4oz) finely chopped candied peel
350g (12oz) each raisins, sultanas and currants
175g (6oz) each light and dark muscovado sugar
1 tbsp ground mixed spice
pinch of freshly grated nutmeg
grated zest and juice of 2 medium oranges
150ml (¼ pint) Calvados

For the almond pastry
225g (8oz) plain flour, plus extra to dust
50g (2oz) ground almonds
75g (3oz) golden icing sugar
175g (6oz) unsalted butter, chilled and diced
2 medium egg yolks

For the shortbread topping
75g (3oz) unsalted butter, softened
25g (1oz) golden caster sugar, plus extra to sprinkle
75g (3oz) plain flour
50g (2oz) ground almonds

1 To make the mincemeat, combine all the ingredients in a large bowl. Put into five 500ml (18fl oz) sterilised jars, seal and label. Leave for at least 24 hours (or up to three months).

2 To make the almond pastry, put the flour, almonds, icing sugar and salt in a food processor and whiz for 30 seconds. Add the butter and whiz until the mixture resembles fine crumbs. Add the egg yolks and whiz until the mixture just comes together (if it's a little dry, add 1–2 tsp cold water). Knead lightly on a floured surface. Wrap in clingfilm and chill for 1 hour.

3 To make the topping, beat the butter and sugar until light, then mix in the flour and almonds to form a dough; wrap and chill for 15 minutes. Line four 12-hole bun tins with paper cake cases.

4 On a lightly floured surface, roll out the pastry to 3mm (⅛in) thick. Stamp out rounds using a 7.5cm (3in) fluted cutter. Put in the paper cases and prick the bases. Chill for 10 minutes. Preheat the oven to 190°C (170°C fan oven) mark 5. Put 1 tbsp mincemeat into each pastry case.

5 Roll out the topping to 3mm (⅛in) thick. Using a small holly cutter, cut and arrange two leaves on each pie. Mark the leaves with veins. Decorate each with two cranberries. Sprinkle with caster sugar. Bake for 12–15 minutes until golden. Cool in the tins for 15 minutes, then cool completely on a wire rack. Store in an airtight container for up to two days.

Makes 48	A LITTLE EFFORT		NUTRITIONAL INFORMATION	
	Preparation Time 45 minutes, plus chilling, plus mincemeat	**Cooking Time** 12–15 minutes, plus cooling	**Per Pie** 190 calories, 6g fat (of which 3g saturates), 33g carbohydrate, 0.1g salt	Vegetarian

Try Something Different

Replace the lemon zest and juice with orange, the cranberries with blueberries and the Brazil nuts with hazelnuts.

Pear and Cranberry Strudel

125g (4oz) fresh cranberries

550g (1¼lb) Williams or Comice pears, cored and sliced

50g (2oz) Brazil nuts, chopped and toasted

grated zest and juice of 1 lemon

25g (1oz) golden caster sugar

1 tbsp fresh white breadcrumbs

1 tsp ground cinnamon

7 sheets filo pastry, thawed if frozen

75g (3oz) butter, melted

icing sugar to dust

1 Preheat the oven to 190°C (170°C fan oven) mark 5. Grease a large baking sheet. Toss the cranberries with the pears, nuts and lemon juice. Mix the lemon zest with 1 tbsp caster sugar, the breadcrumbs and cinnamon; combine with the cranberry mixture.

2 Lay a clean teatowel on a board and put three sheets of filo pastry on it, each overlapping the other by 12.5cm (5in) to make a 56 x 48cm (22 x 19in) rectangle. Brush with melted butter, then put three more sheets on top and brush again.

3 Spoon the pear mixture on to the pastry and roll up from a long edge. Carefully lift on to the baking sheet, placing it seam-side down. Cut the remaining filo pastry into strips, crumple and place on the strudel; brush with melted butter. Sprinkle the strudel with the remaining caster sugar and bake for 40–45 minutes, covering with foil if the top browns too quickly. Dust the strudel with icing sugar. Serve warm.

Serves 8	EASY		NUTRITIONAL INFORMATION	
	Preparation Time 20 minutes	**Cooking Time** 40–45 minutes	**Per Serving** 190 calories, 12g fat (of which 6g saturates), 19g carbohydrate, 0.2g salt	Vegetarian

Spiced Nut Strudel

50g (2oz) glacé cherries, chopped

200g (7oz) mixed chopped nuts, such as walnuts, hazelnuts and almonds

50g (2oz) raisins

50g (2oz) fresh white breadcrumbs

25g (1oz) dark muscovado sugar

25g (1oz) chopped candied peel

1 tsp each ground cinnamon and ground ginger

75g (3oz) unsalted butter

6 tbsp maple syrup, plus extra to drizzle

1 large egg, beaten

8 large sheets filo pastry, thawed if frozen

1 Preheat the oven to 190°C (170°C fan oven) mark 5. Put the cherries in a bowl with the nuts, raisins, breadcrumbs, sugar, candied peel, cinnamon and ginger. Melt 50g (2oz) butter and add to the mixture with the maple syrup and egg. Mix well.

2 Melt the remaining butter. Lay one sheet of filo pastry on a worksurface, then brush it lightly with melted butter. Take a second sheet of filo pastry and position it so that it overlaps the first sheet by 5cm (2in), then brush lightly with melted butter.

3 Spoon half of the strudel filling over the filo pastry, leaving a 5cm (2in) border all round. Lay another two sheets of filo pastry over the filling, brushing them with butter. Spoon the remaining filling on top. Fold the two long edges of the pastry over the edge of the filling. Loosely roll up like a Swiss roll to enclose the filling. Carefully transfer the strudel to a baking sheet, placing it seam-side down. Brush lightly with melted butter.

4 Cut the remaining filo pastry into strips. Crumple the filo strips and arrange them on top of the strudel. Brush with the remaining melted butter and bake for about 30 minutes or until the pastry is a deep golden brown. Drizzle a little maple syrup over and serve warm.

EASY		NUTRITIONAL INFORMATION		Serves
Preparation Time 20 minutes	**Cooking Time** 30 minutes	**Per Serving** 405 calories, 26g fat (of which 7g saturates), 38g carbohydrate, 0.4g salt	Vegetarian	**8**

Try Something Different

For the filling, reduce the currants to 125g (4oz), add 50g (2oz) chopped walnuts and replace the zest of 1 lemon with the zest of 1 small orange.

Citrus Eccles Cakes

Rough Puff Pastry (see page 13)

flour to dust

beaten egg to glaze

50g (2oz) unsalted butter, melted, plus extra to grease

caster sugar to sprinkle

For the filling

175g (6oz) currants

50g (2oz) chopped mixed candied peel

50g (2oz) muscovado sugar

finely grated zest of 2 lemons

1. Preheat the oven to 220°C (200°C fan oven) mark 7. To make the filling, mix all the ingredients together in a bowl.

2. Roll out half the pastry on a lightly floured surface to a 51 x 20.5cm (20 x 8in) rectangle, then cut in half lengthways. Cut each strip crossways into five equal pieces.

3. With the tip of sharp knife, make rows of 2cm ($^3/_4$in) slits on each piece of pastry, spacing them 5mm ($^1/_4$in) apart and staggering alternate rows so that the pastry forms a lattice when pulled apart slightly. Brush the edges with beaten egg.

4. Divide the filling among the latticed pastries, placing it in the centre of each. Bring the edges of the pastry up over the filling, pinching them together to seal. Invert on to a lightly greased baking sheet, so that the neat lattice sides are uppermost.

5. Brush the pastry with beaten egg and sprinkle lightly with caster sugar. Bake for 12–15 minutes until puffed and golden.

6. Pour a little melted butter into each cake, through the lattice. Serve warm.

EASY		NUTRITIONAL INFORMATION		Makes
Preparation Time 35 minutes, plus chilling	**Cooking Time** 12–15 minutes	**Per Cake** 161 calories, 10g fat (of which 6g saturates), 19g carbohydrate, 0.2g salt	Vegetarian	**20**

Pistachio Baklava

175g (6oz) shelled, unsalted pistachio nuts

125g (4oz) pinenuts

1 tsp ground cinnamon

½ tsp ground cloves

a pinch of freshly grated nutmeg

2 tbsp caster sugar

225g (8oz) filo pastry, thawed if frozen

75g (3oz) unsalted butter, melted

For the syrup

grated zest and juice of ½ lemon

225g (8oz) clear honey

2 cardamom pods, bruised

2 tbsp rosewater (optional)

1 Preheat the oven to 180°C (160°C fan oven) mark 4. Put the pistachio nuts, pinenuts, cinnamon, cloves and nutmeg in a food processor and pulse briefly until coarsely ground. Stir in the caster sugar.

2 Brush a sheet of filo pastry with melted butter and press into an 18 x 25.5cm (7 x 10in) baking tin. Continue to brush and layer half the filo. Scatter the nut mixture over, then top with the remaining filo sheets, brushing each with butter. Score through the pastry in a diamond pattern. Drizzle over any remaining butter and bake for 20 minutes. Lower the oven to 170°C (150°C fan oven) mark 3 and bake for a further 20–25 minutes until crisp and golden.

3 To make the syrup, put the lemon zest and juice, honey, cardamom pods and 150ml (¼ pint) water in a pan; simmer gently for 5 minutes. Remove from the heat and stir in the rosewater, if using. Pour half the honey syrup evenly over the hot baklava. Leave in the tin until completely cold. Cut into diamond shapes and drizzle with the remaining syrup.

Serves 8	EASY		NUTRITIONAL INFORMATION	
	Preparation Time 30 minutes	**Cooking Time** 40–45 minutes	**Per Serving** 479 calories, 31g fat (of which 7g saturates), 45g carbohydrate, 0.4g salt	Vegetarian

Try Something Different

Coffee Choux Buns: for the filling, replace the vanilla extract with 2 tsp freshly made and cooled, strong espresso coffee. For the topping, stir 1 tbsp of the same coffee into the melted chocolate and butter, before cooling.

Chocolate Choux Buns

Choux Pastry (see page 14)

For the filling

300ml (½ pint) double cream

1 tsp vanilla extract

1 tsp golden caster sugar

For the topping

200g (7oz) plain chocolate, in pieces

75g (3oz) butter, at room temperature

1 Preheat the oven to 220°C (200°C fan oven) mark 7. Sprinkle a non-stick baking sheet with a little water. Using two dampened tablespoons, spoon the choux paste into eight large mounds on the baking sheet, spacing them well apart to allow room for expansion.

2 Bake for about 30 minutes until risen and golden brown. Make a small hole in the side of each bun, then put back in the switched-off oven for 10–15 minutes to dry out. Transfer to a wire rack and set aside to cool.

3 For the filling, whip the cream with the vanilla extract and sugar until soft peaks form. Split the choux buns and fill them with the cream.

4 For the topping, melt the chocolate with the butter in a heatproof bowl set over a pan of gently simmering water. Leave to cool until beginning to thicken. Top the choux buns with the warm melted chocolate to serve.

EASY		NUTRITIONAL INFORMATION		Makes
Preparation Time 25 minutes	**Cooking Time** 40–45 minutes, plus cooling	**Per Bun** 475 calories, 40g fat (of which 25g saturates), 25g carbohydrate, 0.3g salt	Vegetarian	**8**

4

Classic Sweet Tarts

Try Something Different

Chocolate Custard Tart: replace 25g (1oz) of the flour with sifted cocoa powder. For the custard, omit the vanilla pod, and heat 375ml (13fl oz) single cream with 100g (3½oz) chopped plain chocolate (70% cocoa solids), until melted and just simmering.

Vanilla Egg Custard Tart

Sweet Shortcrust Pastry (see page 12), made with 175g (6oz) plain flour, 125g (4oz) butter, 25g (1oz) vanilla sugar, 1 tsp grated orange zest and 1 medium egg yolk

flour to dust

175g (6oz) raspberries (optional) to serve

vanilla sugar to dust

For the vanilla custard

2 large eggs

2 large egg yolks

40g (1½oz) golden caster sugar

450ml (¾ pint) single cream

½ vanilla pod, split lengthways

1 Roll out the pastry on a lightly floured surface and use to line a 20.5cm (8in), 4cm (1½in) deep, loose-based fluted tart tin. Chill for 30 minutes.

2 Preheat the oven to 200°C (180°C fan oven) mark 6. Bake the pastry case blind (see page 16).

3 Meanwhile, make the vanilla custard. Put the whole eggs, egg yolks and sugar into a bowl and beat well. Put the cream and vanilla pod into a small pan over a very low heat until the cream is almost boiling. Pour on to the egg mixture, whisking constantly, then strain into the pastry case.

4 Reduce the oven temperature to 150°C (130°C fan oven) mark 2 and put the tart in the oven. Bake for 45 minutes until the centre is softly set. Leave until cold, then carefully remove from the tin. Top with raspberries if you like, and dust with vanilla sugar.

Serves 6	EASY		NUTRITIONAL INFORMATION	
	Preparation Time 40 minutes, plus 1 hour chilling	**Cooking Time** 1 hour, plus cooling	**Per Serving** 497 calories, 36g fat (of which 21g saturates), 36g carbohydrate, 0.4g salt	Vegetarian

Try Something Different

For the pastry, replace half the plain flour with wholemeal flour. For the filling, use fresh wholemeal breadcrumbs instead of white.

Sweet Shortcrust Pastry (see page 12), made with 225g (8oz) plain flour, 150g (5oz) unsalted butter, 15g (½oz) golden caster sugar and 1 medium egg yolk

flour to dust

For the filling

700g (1½lb) golden syrup

175g (6oz) fresh white breadcrumbs

grated zest of 3 lemons

2 medium eggs, lightly beaten

Treacle Tart

1 Preheat the oven to 180°C (160°C fan oven) mark 4. Roll out the pastry on a lightly floured surface and use to line a 25.5cm (10in), 4cm (1½in) deep, loose-based fluted tart tin. Prick the base with a fork.

2 To make the filling, heat the golden syrup in a pan over a low heat until thinned in consistency. Remove from the heat and mix in the breadcrumbs and lemon zest. Stir in the beaten eggs.

3 Pour the filling into the pastry case and bake for 45–50 minutes until the filling is lightly set and golden. Allow to cool slightly. Serve warm.

EASY		NUTRITIONAL INFORMATION		Serves
Preparation Time 25 minutes, plus 30 minutes chilling	**Cooking Time** 45–50 minutes, plus cooling	**Per Serving** 486 calories, 15g fat (of which 8g saturates), 88g carbohydrate, 1.1g salt	Vegetarian	**6**

Cook's Tips

Remember that oven temperatures vary, so check the tart after 15 minutes of cooking. Turn round if cooking unevenly, otherwise the eggs might curdle.

To freeze Complete the recipe, cool, wrap and freeze for up to three months.

To use Thaw for 3 hours at room temperature. Decorate and serve.

Classic Lemon Tart

butter to grease

flour to dust

Sweet Shortcrust Pastry (see page 12), made with 150g (5oz) plain flour, 75g (3oz) unsalted butter, 50g (2oz) icing sugar and 2 large egg yolks

peach slices and fresh or frozen raspberries, thawed, to decorate

icing sugar to dust

For the filling

1 large egg, plus 4 large yolks

150g (5oz) caster sugar

grated zest of 4 lemons

150ml (¼ pint) freshly squeezed lemon juice (about 4 medium lemons)

150ml (¼ pint) double cream

1   Grease and flour a 23cm (9in), 2.5cm (1in) deep, loose-based flan tin. On a lightly floured surface, roll out the pastry into a circle – if the pastry sticks to the surface, gently ease a palette knife under it to loosen. Line the tin with the pastry and trim the excess. Chill for 30 minutes.

2   Preheat the oven to 190°C (170°C fan oven) mark 5. Put the tin on a baking sheet and bake the pastry case blind (see page 16). Reduce the oven temperature to 170°C (150°C fan oven) mark 3.

3   Meanwhile, to make the filling, put the whole egg, egg yolks and caster sugar in a bowl and beat together with a wooden spoon or balloon whisk until smooth. Carefully stir in the lemon zest, lemon juice and cream. Leave to stand for 5 minutes.

4   Ladle three-quarters of filling into the pastry case, position the baking sheet on the oven shelf and ladle in the remainder. Bake for 25–30 minutes until the filling bounces back when touched lightly in the centre. Cool for 15 minutes to serve warm, or cool completely and chill. Decorate with peaches and raspberries and dust with icing sugar.

Serves 8	EASY		NUTRITIONAL INFORMATION	
	Preparation Time 30 minutes, plus 1 hour chilling	**Cooking Time** 50 minutes, plus cooling	**Per Serving** 385 calories, 23g fat (of which 13g saturates), 42g carbohydrate, 0.2g salt	Vegetarian

Cook's Tip

When caramelising the apples in step 2, be patient. Allow the sauce to turn a dark golden brown – any paler and it will be too sickly. Don't let it burn, though, as this will make the caramel taste bitter.

Sweet Shortcrust Pastry (see page 12), made with 225g (8oz) plain flour, ¼ tsp salt, 150g (5oz) unsalted butter, 50g (2oz) golden icing sugar, 1 medium egg and 2–3 drops vanilla extract

flour to dust

For the topping

200g (7oz) golden caster sugar

125g (4oz) chilled unsalted butter

1.4–1.6kg (3–3½lb) crisp dessert apples, peeled and cored

juice of ½ lemon

Tarte Tatin

1 To make the topping, sprinkle the caster sugar over the base of a 20.5cm (8in) tarte tatin tin or ovenproof frying pan. Cut the butter into slivers and arrange on the sugar. Halve the apples and pack them tightly, cut side up, on top of the butter.

2 Put the tin or pan on the hob and cook over a medium heat for 30 minutes (making sure it doesn't bubble over or catch on the bottom) until the butter and sugar turn a dark golden brown (see Cook's Tip). Sprinkle with the lemon juice, then allow to cool for 15 minutes. Meanwhile, preheat the oven to 220°C (200°C fan oven) mark 7.

3 Put the pastry on a large sheet of baking parchment. Roll out the pastry to make a round 2.5cm (1in) larger than the tin or pan. Prick several times with a fork. Lay the pastry over the apples, tucking the edges down the side of the tin. Bake for 25–30 minutes until golden brown. Leave in the tin for 10 minutes, then carefully upturn on to a serving plate. Serve warm.

Serves 6	EASY		NUTRITIONAL INFORMATION	
	Preparation Time 30 minutes, plus 30 minutes chilling	**Cooking Time** about 1 hour, plus cooling	**Per Serving** 727 calories, 39g fat (of which 24g saturates), 94g carbohydrate, 0.7g salt	Vegetarian

Try Something Different

Replace the pears with 3-4 bananas, thickly sliced on the diagonal. Cook the dulce de leche for 5 minutes in step 1, stir in the bananas to coat, then arrange in the tin in an overlapping circle. Complete the recipe.

Easy Pear and Toffee Tarte Tatin

4 small rosy pears, quartered and cored – no need to peel them

8 tbsp dulce de leche toffee sauce

225g (8oz) ready-rolled puff pastry

flour to dust

cream or vanilla ice cream to serve

1 Preheat the oven to 200°C (180°C fan oven) mark 6. Put the pears and toffee sauce in a large non-stick frying pan. Cook over a medium heat for 5 minutes or until the pears are well coated and the sauce has turned a slightly darker shade of golden brown.

2 Tip the pears and sauce into a 20.5cm (8in) non-stick sandwich or tart tin. Arrange the pears skin side down in a circle and leave to cool for 10 minutes.

3 If necessary, roll out the puff pastry on a lightly floured surface until it is wide enough to cover the tin. Lay it over the pears and press down on to the edge of the tin. Trim off any excess pastry. Prick the pastry all over, then bake for 20–25 minutes until well risen and golden.

4 Leave to cool for 5 minutes. To turn out, hold a large serving plate or baking sheet over the tart, turn over and give a quick shake to loosen. Lift off the tin. Serve the tart immediately, cut into wedges, with cream or ice cream.

EASY		NUTRITIONAL INFORMATION		Serves
Preparation Time 15 minutes	**Cooking Time** 25–30 minutes	**Per Serving** 294 calories, 12g fat (of which 2g saturates), 46g carbohydrate, 0.5g salt	Vegetarian	**6**

Cook's Tip

Serve within 2 hours of putting the pie together, otherwise the pastry will go soggy.

Strawberry Tart

Sweet Shortcrust Pastry (see page 12), made with 125g (4oz) plain flour, a pinch of salt, 50g (2oz) golden caster sugar, 50g (2oz) butter and 2 medium egg yolks

flour to dust

For the crème pâtissière

300ml (½ pint) milk

1 vanilla pod, split and seeds separated

2 medium egg yolks

50g (2oz) golden caster sugar

2 tbsp plain flour

2 tbsp cornflour

50ml (2fl oz) crème fraîche

For the topping

450g (1lb) medium strawberries, hulled and halved

6 tbsp redcurrant jelly

Try Something Different

Replace the strawberries with a mixture of raspberries, blueberries, redcurrants and blackcurrants.

1 To make the crème pâtissière, put the milk in a pan with the vanilla pod and seeds. Heat gently to just below boiling, then remove from the heat. Put the yolks and sugar in a bowl, beat until pale, then stir in the flours. Discard the vanilla pod, then gradually mix the hot milk into the yolk mixture. Return to the pan and slowly bring to the boil, stirring, for 3–4 minutes until thick and smooth. Scrape into a bowl, cover with a circle of damp greaseproof paper. Cool.

2 Put the pastry between two sheets of greaseproof paper and roll out thinly. Use to line a 23cm (9in) loose-based flan tin. Prick with a fork, line with greaseproof paper and chill for 30 minutes. Preheat the oven to 190°C (170°C fan oven) mark 5. Fill the case with baking beans and bake for 10–15 minutes. Remove the paper and beans, put back in the oven and bake for 10 minutes until golden. Cool for 5 minutes, then remove from the tin and cool completely.

3 Add the crème fraîche to the crème pâtissière and beat until smooth. Spread evenly in the pastry case. Arrange the strawberry halves on top, working from the outside edge into the centre.

4 Heat the redcurrant jelly in a pan until syrupy, whisking lightly. Using a pastry brush, cover the strawberries with jelly. Serve within 2 hours.

EASY			NUTRITIONAL INFORMATION		Serves
Preparation Time 40 minutes, plus 1 hour chilling	**Cooking Time** 35–40 minutes, plus cooling		**Per Serving** 384 calories, 15g fat (of which 8g saturates), 57g carbohydrate, 0.2g salt	Vegetarian	**6**

Freezing Tip

Bake the tarts, then cool, wrap and freeze.
To use Put back in the tins, then thaw overnight at room temperature. Reheat at 200°C (180°C fan oven) mark 6 for 7–10 minutes.

3 medium eggs

a pinch of salt

300g (11oz) plain flour, plus extra to dust

75g (3oz) icing sugar

175g (6oz) butter

For the filling

700g (1½lb) Bramley or Granny Smith's apples, peeled, cored and thinly sliced

grated zest and juice of 2 lemons

150g (5oz) butter

225g (8oz) caster sugar, plus extra to dust

1 tsp arrowroot

Apple and Lemon Tartlets

1 Beat one egg with a pinch of salt then set aside 1 tbsp. Whiz the flour, icing sugar and butter in a food processor until the mixture resembles fine crumbs. Add the remaining beaten egg with 3 tbsp water; pulse until the pastry comes together. Divide into eight balls and chill for 30 minutes. Roll out on a lightly floured surface and line eight 8cm (3¼in) loose-based fluted tartlet tins. Prick with a fork and chill for 20 minutes. Preheat the oven to 200°C (180°C fan oven) mark 6. Bake blind (see page 16). Reduce the oven temperature to 180°C (160°C fan oven) mark 4.

2 Toss the apples in 2 tbsp lemon juice. Fry in 25g (1oz) butter for 1–2 minutes. Spoon into the pastry cases. Process the remaining butter with the caster sugar for 3 minutes until pale. Add the arrowroot, lemon zest and remaining 2 eggs; blend for 2 minutes. With the food processor running, add the remaining lemon juice; blend for 1 minute. Pour over the apples. Dust with caster sugar and bake for 45–50 minutes until the apples start to caramelise. Serve warm or cold.

Serves 8	EASY		NUTRITIONAL INFORMATION	
	Preparation Time 40 minutes, plus 50 minutes chilling	**Cooking Time** 45–50 minutes	**Per Serving** 615 calories, 34g fat (of which 20g saturates), 77g carbohydrate, 0.6g salt	Vegetarian

150g (5oz) butter, chilled and diced
175g (6oz) plain flour, plus extra to dust
7 tbsp soured cream

For the topping
50g (2oz) butter
50g (2oz) caster sugar, plus extra to dust
2 medium eggs, lightly beaten
100g (3½oz) ground almonds
1 tbsp Kirsch or 3–4 drops almond essence
900g (2lb) plums, stoned and quartered
50g (2oz) blanched almonds to decorate
175g (6oz) redcurrant jelly

Plum and Almond Tart

1 To make the pastry, put the butter in a food processor with the flour and whiz for 1–2 seconds. Add the soured cream and process for a further 1–2 seconds until the dough just begins to come together. Turn out on to a lightly floured surface and knead lightly for about 30 seconds or until the pastry just comes together. Wrap in clingfilm and chill for 30 minutes.

2 To make the topping, put the butter in a bowl and beat until soft, then add the sugar and beat until light and fluffy. Beat in the eggs, alternating with the ground almonds. Add the Kirsch or almond essence, cover and set aside.

3 Roll out the pastry to a 30.5cm (12in) circle, then transfer to a baking sheet and prick with a fork. Spread the almond mixture over the pastry, leaving a 3cm (1¼in) border all round. Scatter over the plums and fold the edges of the pastry up over the fruit. Dust with caster sugar, then chill for 20 minutes.

4 Preheat the oven to 220°C (200°C fan oven) mark 7 and put a baking tray in the oven to heat for 10 minutes. Put the tart on its baking sheet on top of the hot baking tray. Cook for 35–40 minutes until deep golden brown.

5 Leave the tart to cool for 10 minutes, then slide it on to a wire rack. Arrange the almonds among the fruit. Heat the redcurrant jelly gently in a pan, stirring until smooth, then brush generously over the tart. Leave to set.

EASY		NUTRITIONAL INFORMATION		Serves
Preparation Time 30 minutes, plus 30 minutes chilling	**Cooking Time** 40 minutes, plus cooling	**Per Serving** 535 calories, 35g fat (of which 16g saturates), 50g carbohydrate, 0.5g salt	Vegetarian	**8**

Try Something Different

Replace the prunes with ready-to-eat dried apricots. Soak in 2½ tbsp Amaretto liqueur and 2½ tbsp water instead of brandy.

Glazed Brandied Prune Tart

Sweet Shortcrust Pastry (see page 12), made with 175g (6oz) plain flour, 75g (3oz) caster sugar, 75g (3oz) butter and 3 large egg yolks

flour to dust

For the filling

250g (9oz) ready-to-eat pitted prunes

5 tbsp brandy

1 vanilla pod, split

150ml (¼ pint) double cream

150ml (¼ pint) single cream

25g (1oz) caster sugar

2 large eggs

4 tbsp apricot jam and 2 tbsp brandy to glaze

1 To make the filling, put the prunes into a small bowl, add the brandy, then cover and leave to soak overnight or for several hours.

2 Roll out the pastry on a lightly floured surface and use to line a 23cm (9in), 2.5cm (1in) deep, loose-based fluted flan tin. Chill for 30 minutes. Preheat the oven to 200°C (180°C fan oven) mark 6.

3 Prick the pastry base with a fork, then bake blind (see page 16). Reduce the oven temperature to 180°C (160°C fan oven) mark 4.

4 Meanwhile, put the vanilla pod in a pan with the double cream. Bring just to the boil, then remove from the heat and set aside to infuse for 20 minutes.

5 Remove the vanilla pod, rinse, dry and store for reuse. Pour the infused cream into a bowl, then add the single cream, sugar and eggs. Beat well.

6 Scatter the prunes over the pastry case, then pour the cream mixture around them. Bake for 30 minutes or until the custard is turning golden and is just set in the centre.

7 Meanwhile, sieve the jam into a pan, add the brandy and heat gently until smooth. Brush the glaze over the tart and serve warm or cold.

	EASY		NUTRITIONAL INFORMATION	
Serves **8**	**Preparation Time** 25 minutes, plus overnight soaking, plus chilling	**Cooking Time** 50 minutes	**Per Serving** 440 calories, 24g fat (of which 14g saturates), 47g carbohydrate, 0.2g salt	Vegetarian

Sweet Shortcrust Pastry (see page 12), made with 200g (7oz) plain flour, 75g (3oz) unsalted butter, 50g (2oz) golden caster sugar and 1 medium egg

flour to dust

For the filling

100g (3¹/₂oz) cracked wheat or bulgur wheat

200ml (7fl oz) milk

250g (9oz) ricotta cheese

150g (5oz) golden caster sugar

2 medium eggs

1 tbsp orange flower water

1 tsp vanilla extract

¹/₂ tsp ground cinnamon

1 piece – about 40g (1¹/₂oz) – candied peel, finely chopped

icing sugar to dust

Sweet Ricotta Tart

1 To make the filling, put the cracked or bulgur wheat in a pan, add the milk, then cover and bring to the boil. Turn down the heat and simmer for 5–8 minutes until all the liquid has been absorbed and the wheat still has a slight bite. Leave to cool.

2 Preheat the oven to 190°C (170°C fan oven) mark 5. Roll out the pastry on a lightly floured surface and use to line a 20.5cm (8in) loose-based sandwich tin. Cover and chill for 10 minutes. Knead together the trimmings, then wrap and chill. Bake the pastry blind (see page 16).

3 Put the ricotta in a bowl and add the sugar, eggs, orange flower water, vanilla extract and cinnamon. Beat well. Add the peel and cracked wheat, and mix.

4 Roll out the pastry trimmings and cut out six strips each measuring 1 x 20.5cm (¹/₂ x 8in). Pour the filling into the pastry case and lay the strips on top. Bake for 45 minutes. Leave in the tin for 10 minutes, then cool on a wire rack. Dust with icing sugar to serve.

Serves 8	EASY		NUTRITIONAL INFORMATION	
	Preparation Time 25 minutes, plus 40 minutes chilling	**Cooking Time** 1 hour, plus cooling	**Per Serving** 404 calories, 15g fat (of which 9g saturates), 60g carbohydrate, 0.3g salt	Vegetarian

250g (9oz) plain flour
200g (7oz) unsalted butter, softened
40g (1½oz) icing sugar
4 large eggs
100g (3½oz) pinenuts
200g (7oz) muscovado sugar
100ml (3½fl oz) clear honey
150ml (¼ pint) double cream
Yogurt Ice Cream to serve (see page 20)

Pinenut and Honey Tart

1 Pulse 225g (8oz) flour, 150g (5oz) butter and the icing sugar in a food processor until the mixture resembles fine crumbs. (Alternatively, rub the butter into the flour in a large bowl by hand or using a pastry cutter until it resembles fine crumbs. Stir in the icing sugar.) Add one egg. Pulse, or stir with a fork, until the mixture forms a ball. Wrap in clingfilm and chill for 30 minutes. Preheat the oven to 200°C (180°C fan oven) mark 6.

2 Roll out the pastry and use to line a 23cm (9in) loose-based tart tin. Prick with a fork and bake blind (see page 16). Increase the oven temperature to 190°C (170°C fan oven) mark 5.

3 Sprinkle 75g (3oz) pinenuts over the pastry base. Melt 25g (1oz) butter and whisk with 175g (6oz) muscovado sugar, the honey, remaining eggs and the cream. Pour into the pastry case and bake for 25–30 minutes.

4 Pulse the remaining pinenuts, flour, butter and sugar until the mixture forms a crumble texture. (Alternatively, rub the butter into the flour in a large bowl and stir in the pinenuts and sugar.) When the tart is cooked, remove it from the oven, sprinkle with the crumble mixture and return to the oven for 8–10 minutes. Leave to cool slightly. Serve warm with Yogurt Ice Cream.

EASY		NUTRITIONAL INFORMATION		Serves
Preparation Time 50 minutes, plus chilling	**Cooking Time** 1 hour, plus cooling	**Per Serving** 863 calories, 54g fat (of which 26g saturates), 88g carbohydrate, 0.6g salt	Vegetarian	**6**

Try Something Different

Omit the orange zest and replace the Grand Marnier with crème de menthe.

Chocolate Orange Tart

Sweet Shortcrust Pastry (see page 12), made with 150g (5oz) plain flour, a pinch of salt, 75g (3oz) unsalted butter, 25g (1oz) golden icing sugar, grated zest of 1 orange and 2 large egg yolks

flour to dust

icing sugar to dust

For the filling

175g (6oz) plain chocolate (at least 50% cocoa solids), chopped

175ml (6fl oz) double cream

75g (3oz) light muscovado sugar

2 medium eggs

1 tbsp Grand Marnier or Cointreau

1 Roll out the pastry on a lightly floured surface and use to line a 20.5cm (8in) loose-based tart tin. Prick with a fork, put the tin on a baking sheet and chill for 30 minutes. Preheat the oven to 190°C (170°C fan oven) mark 5.

2 Bake the pastry case blind (see page 16). Remove from the oven and put to one side. Reduce the oven temperature to 170°C (150°C fan oven) mark 3.

3 To make the filling, melt the chocolate in a heatproof bowl set over a pan of gently simmering water. Leave to cool for 10 minutes.

4 Put the cream, muscovado sugar, eggs and liqueur into a bowl and stir, using a wooden spoon to mix thoroughly. Gradually stir in the chocolate, then pour into the pastry case and bake for 20 minutes until just set. Serve warm or cold, dusted liberally with icing sugar.

Serves 8	EASY		NUTRITIONAL INFORMATION	
	Preparation Time 30 minutes, plus 1 hour chilling	**Cooking Time** about 1 hour, plus cooling	**Per Serving** 441 calories, 28g fat (of which 17g saturates), 42g carbohydrate, 0.2g salt	Vegetarian

Cook's Tip

Plum Sauce: put 450g (1lb) ripe plums, halved and stoned, 50–75g (2–3oz) soft brown sugar and 150ml (¼ pint) sweet white wine in a pan with 150ml (¼ pint) water. Bring to the boil, then simmer until tender. Remove 3 plums to decorate; slice and put to one side. Cook the remaining plums until very soft, about 15 minutes. Put in a food processor and process until smooth. Sieve, if you like, adding more sugar to taste. Cool.

Almond Bakewell Tarts

1 Preheat the oven to 190°C (170°C fan oven) mark 5. Roll out the pastry thinly on a lightly floured surfact and line six 10cm (4in), 3cm (1¼in) deep tartlet tins. Prick with a fork and bake blind (see page 16). Cool.

2 To make the filling, beat the butter and sugar together until light and fluffy. Gradually beat in 2 eggs, then beat in the remaining egg with one-third of the ground almonds. Fold in the remaining almonds and the almond essence.

3 Melt the redcurrant jelly in a small pan and brush over the insides of the pastry cases. Spoon in the almond filling. Put the tarts on a baking sheet and bake for 20–25 minutes until golden and just firm. Leave in the tins for 10 minutes, unmould and cool.

4 To make the crumble topping, rub the butter into the flour and add the sugar. Spread evenly on a baking sheet and grill until golden. Cool, then sprinkle over the tarts. Decorate with plums and serve with Plum Sauce.

Sweet Shortcrust Pastry (see page 12), made with 200g (7oz) plain flour, 100g (3½oz) butter, 75g (3oz) caster sugar, 3 large egg yolks and ½ tsp vanilla extract

flour to dust

Plum Sauce (see Cook's Tip) to serve

For the filling
125g (4oz) butter, softened

125g (4oz) caster sugar

3 large eggs

125g (4oz) ground almonds

2–3 drops almond essence

6 tbsp redcurrant jelly

For the crumble topping
25g (1oz) butter

75g (3oz) plain flour

25g (1oz) caster sugar

EASY		NUTRITIONAL INFORMATION		Serves
Preparation Time 25 minutes, plus 30 minutes chilling	**Cooking Time** 50 minutes, plus cooling	**Per Serving** 931 calories, 52g fat (of which 24g saturates), 104g carbohydrate, 0.8g salt	Vegetarian	**6**

5

Indulgent Dessert Tarts

White Chocolate Fruit Tarts

Sweet Shortcrust Pastry (see page 12), made with 225g (8oz) plain flour, 150g (5oz) butter, 50g (2oz) icing sugar, 1 large egg and 2–3 drops vanilla extract

450g (1lb) fresh mango, peeled, stoned and sliced

flour to dust

fresh mint sprigs to decorate

icing sugar to dust

For the filling

275g (10oz) white chocolate, chopped

300ml (½ pint) double cream

1 vanilla pod, split

2 large eggs, separated

2 tbsp Kirsch

Cook's Tips

Don't worry if the pastry cracks when you're lining the tins – it's easy to patch together.

If the filling starts to get too dark during cooking, cover it with foil.

Try other fresh fruits as the topping for these tarts, such as raspberries, halved strawberries and sliced ripe pears.

1   Roll out the pastry thinly on a lightly floured surface and use to line eight 9cm (3½in), 3cm (1¼in) deep, loose-based tartlet tins (see Cook's Tips). Prick with a fork and chill for 30 minutes. Preheat the oven to 200°C (180°C fan oven) mark 6. Bake blind (see page 16). Cool slightly.

2   To make the filling, put the chocolate into a heatproof bowl. Pour the cream into a small, heavy-based pan with the vanilla pod and bring to the boil. Remove from the heat, lift out the vanilla pod and add the hot cream to the chocolate. Stir until the chocolate is completely melted. Cool.

3   Preheat the oven to 190°C (170°C fan oven) mark 5. Mix the egg yolks and the Kirsch into the cooled chocolate and cream mixture. Whisk the egg whites until they form soft peaks, then fold carefully into the chocolate mixture until well incorporated. Pour the mixture into the pastry cases and bake for 10–15 minutes until just set (see Cook's Tips). Leave to cool in the tins and chill for 5 hours or overnight. Don't worry if the filling seems very soft – it will become firmer as it chills.

4   Remove the tarts from the refrigerator 30 minutes before serving. Unmould the tarts and arrange the mango slices on top. Decorate with fresh mint sprigs and dust with icing sugar just before serving.

Serves 8	EASY		NUTRITIONAL INFORMATION	
	Preparation Time 40 minutes, plus 1 hour chilling	**Cooking Time** 40 minutes, plus cooling	**Per Serving** 688 calories, 48g fat (of which 29g saturates), 58g carbohydrate, 0.5g salt	Vegetarian

Cook's Tip

Caramelised Fruit: cut 2 clementines into thick slices and arrange on a non-stick baking sheet. Put 150g (5oz) caster sugar in a small, heavy-based pan. Cook over a low heat until the sugar begins to dissolve, then turn up the heat and cook to a pale caramel. Cool a little and drizzle over the fruit. Allow to set. (The caramel will stay brittle for 1–2 hours.)

Cinnamon Custard Tart

Sweet Shortcrust Pastry (see page 12), made with 250g (9oz) plain flour, 100g (3½oz) butter, 100g (3½oz) icing sugar and 1 large egg

flour to dust

450ml (¾ pint) milk

300ml (½ pint) double cream

1 vanilla pod, split

1 cinnamon stick, crumbled

3 large eggs, lightly whisked

150g (5oz) caster sugar

Caramelised Fruit (see Cook's Tip) to serve

1 Roll out the pastry on a lightly floured surface and use to line a 23cm (9in) loose-based tart tin. Prick with a fork and chill for 30 minutes. Preheat the oven to 200°C (180°C fan oven) mark 6. Bake the pastry case blind (see page 16). Reduce the oven temperature to 150°C (130°C fan oven) mark 2.

2 Bring the milk, cream, vanilla and cinnamon slowly to the boil. Leave to infuse for 20 minutes. Mix the whisked eggs with the caster sugar. Stir the milk into the egg mixture, strain into a jug and pour into the tart. Cook for 40–50 minutes until the filling has just set. Turn the oven off and leave the tart in the oven for 15 minutes. Remove and cool in the tin for 20–30 minutes. Transfer to a wire rack to cool.

3 Slice the tart and spoon the Caramelised Fruit over the top to serve.

Serves	EASY		NUTRITIONAL INFORMATION	
	Preparation Time	**Cooking Time**	**Per Serving**	
8	50 minutes, plus 1 hour chilling	1½ hours, plus cooling	664 calories, 34g fat (of which 20g saturates), 87g carbohydrate, 0.4g salt	Vegetarian

Cook's Tip

Candied Orange Zest: dissolve 50g (2oz) golden caster sugar in a pan with 300ml (½ pint) water. Add the pared zest of 1 orange, cut into slivers. Simmer for 10–15 minutes until the liquid has reduced and the zest is tender. Drain well.

Caramelised Orange Tart

1 To make the filling, put the juices, orange zest, butter, sugar and eggs in a heavy-based pan and heat gently, stirring, until thickened. Stir in the almonds, liqueur and food colouring, if using. Set aside.

2 Preheat the oven to 200°C (180°C fan oven) mark 6. Roll out the pastry on a lightly floured surface and use to line a 23cm (9in) fluted tin. Prick with a fork. Cover and chill for 10 minutes. Bake blind (see page 16). Reduce the oven temperature to 180°C (160°C fan oven) mark 4.

3 Pour the filling into the pastry case and bake for 20 minutes or until just firm. Cool.

4 Sprinkle the sugar over the tart. Caramelise under a preheated hot grill; cool. Spoon the Candied Orange Zest around the edge.

Sweet Shortcrust Pastry (see page 12), made with 225g (8oz) plain flour, a pinch of salt, 125g (4oz) butter, 2 tbsp golden icing sugar and 1 medium egg yolk

flour to dust

40g (1½oz) golden caster sugar to sprinkle

Candied Orange Zest (see Cook's Tip) to decorate

For the filling
juice of 1 lemon

grated zest of 2 oranges and juice of 1 orange

75g (3oz) butter

225g (8oz) golden granulated sugar

3 medium eggs, beaten

75g (3oz) ground almonds

2 tbsp orange liqueur

a few drops of orange food colouring (optional)

EASY			**NUTRITIONAL INFORMATION**		Serves 8
Preparation Time 15 minutes, plus 40 minutes chilling	**Cooking Time** 45 minutes, plus cooling		**Per Serving** 556 calories, 29g fat (of which 14g saturates), 70g carbohydrate, 0.5g salt	Vegetarian	

Try Something Different

Replace the mangoes with 1 small pineapple, peeled, cored and thinly sliced, and the orange juice with pineapple juice.

Coconut and Mango Tart

125g (4oz) plain flour, plus extra to dust

75g (3oz) firm, unsalted butter

1 tbsp caster sugar

40g (1½oz) desiccated coconut

1 medium egg yolk

toasted coconut shreds to decorate

icing sugar to dust

For the filling

2 small ripe mangoes, peeled, stoned and thinly sliced

75ml (2½fl oz) freshly squeezed orange juice

2 tbsp caster sugar, plus 75g (3oz)

3 medium eggs

15g (½oz) cornflour

400ml can coconut milk

150ml (¼ pint) double cream

1 To make the pastry, whiz the flour and butter in a food processor until the mixture resembles fine crumbs. Stir in the caster sugar and coconut. Add the egg yolk and about 2 tbsp cold water and pulse to make a firm dough. Knead lightly, wrap and chill for 30 minutes. Preheat the oven to 200°C (180°C fan oven) mark 6. Roll out the pastry on a lightly floured surface and use to line a 23cm (9in), 4cm (1½in) deep, loose-based flan tin. Bake blind (see page 16). Reduce the oven temperature to 150°C (130°C fan oven) mark 2.

2 Meanwhile, to make the filling, put the mango slices in a heavy-based pan with the orange juice and 2 tbsp caster sugar. Bring to a simmer and cook gently for 3–5 minutes until the mango slices are softened but still retain their shape. Cool slightly.

3 Beat the eggs and the remaining sugar together in a bowl. Blend the cornflour with a little of the coconut milk in a pan. Add the remaining coconut milk and bring to the boil, stirring until thickened. Remove from the heat and stir in the cream. Pour over the egg mixture, stirring until smooth.

4 Drain the mangoes, reserving the juice, and arrange in the pastry case. Stir the reserved juice into the coconut custard and ladle it over the mangoes. Bake for about 30 minutes until the custard is just set; it will continue to firm up as it cools. Leave to cool, then chill for several hours or overnight. Decorate with coconut shreds and dust with icing sugar.

EASY		NUTRITIONAL INFORMATION		Serves
Preparation Time 35 minutes, plus 3-4 hours chilling	**Cooking Time** 50 minutes, plus cooling	**Per Serving** 253 calories, 18g fat (of which 11g saturates), 20g carbohydrate, 0.3g salt	Vegetarian	10

Chocolate and Cherry Amaretti Tart

150g (5oz) butter, softened

50g (2oz) icing sugar, plus extra to dust

1 small egg, beaten

225g (8oz) plain flour, plus extra to dust

For the filling

400g (14oz) pitted bottled or canned morello cherries, drained

3 tbsp brandy, sloe gin or Amaretto liqueur

100g (3½oz) plain chocolate, in pieces

125g (4oz) butter, softened

125g (4oz) golden caster sugar

3 large eggs, beaten

125g (4oz) ground almonds

25g (1oz) self-raising flour, sifted

50g (2oz) amaretti biscuits, finely crushed

75g (3oz) slivered or flaked almonds

1 To make the filling, put the cherries in a bowl and pour on the brandy, sloe gin or liqueur. Cover and set aside for 30 minutes.

2 Meanwhile, make the pastry. Whiz the butter, icing sugar and egg in a food processor until almost smooth. Add the flour and process until the mixture just begins to form a dough. Knead the pastry lightly, then wrap in clingfilm and chill for 30 minutes.

3 Roll out the pastry on a lightly floured surface and use to line a 23cm (9in) loose-based fluted flan tin. Chill for 30 minutes. Preheat the oven to 200°C (180°C fan oven) mark 6.

4 Bake the pastry case blind (see page 16). Reduce the oven temperature to 150°C (130°C fan oven) mark 2.

5 Melt the chocolate in a heatproof bowl over a pan of gently simmering water. Stir until smooth, then set aside to cool. In a bowl, beat together the butter and sugar until pale and fluffy. Gradually beat in the eggs, alternating with the ground almonds and flour. Finally, fold in the cooled melted chocolate and crushed amaretti.

6 Spoon about one third of the mixture over the base of the pastry case. Spoon the cherries evenly over the surface, then top with the remaining filling mixture and spread out carefully to cover the cherries. Sprinkle the almonds over the surface and bake for about 1 hour. The tart will have a thin crust on top, but be quite soft underneath.

7 Leave the tart in the tin for 10–15 minutes to firm up, then carefully unmould and dust with icing sugar. Serve warm.

Serves 8	EASY		NUTRITIONAL INFORMATION	
	Preparation Time 30 minutes, plus 50 minutes chilling	**Cooking Time** 1¼ hours, plus cooling	**Per Serving** 760 calories, 50g fat (of which 22g saturates), 67g carbohydrate, 0.8g salt	Vegetarian

Almond and White Chocolate Tart with Pineapple

Sweet Shortcrust Pastry (see page 12), made with 175g (6oz) plain flour, 50g (2oz) icing sugar, 75g (3oz) butter, grated zest of 1 large orange and 1 large egg yolk

flour to dust

For the filling

100g (3½oz) white chocolate, in pieces

125g (4oz) butter

125g (4oz) icing sugar

2 large eggs, beaten

125g (4oz) ground almonds

1 tbsp plain flour

a few drops of vanilla extract

For the topping

1 medium pineapple, peeled and thinly sliced

icing sugar to sprinkle

125g (4oz) apricot jam

1 Roll out the pastry thinly on a lightly floured surface and line a 23cm (9in), 2.5cm (1in) deep, loose-based fluted tart tin. Chill for 20 minutes. Preheat the oven to 200°C (180°C fan oven) mark 6.

2 Prick the pastry base with a fork, then bake blind (see page 16). Reduce the oven temperature to 180°C (160°C fan oven) mark 4.

3 To make the filling, melt the chocolate in a heatproof bowl over a pan of gently simmering water. Cool slightly. Put the butter in a large bowl, beat until creamy with an electric hand whisk and beat in the icing sugar until fluffy. Gradually beat the eggs into the butter mixture, a little at a time. Stir in the ground almonds, flour, melted chocolate and vanilla extract. Fill the pastry case with the mixture and smooth the top. Bake for 25–30 minutes until just set in the middle. The mixture will puff in the oven and firm up on cooling. Cool for 15 minutes, then transfer to a wire rack.

4 For the topping, sprinkle the pineapple heavily with icing sugar and put under a hot grill until the pineapple is glazed to a light caramel colour. Cool. Put the jam in a small pan and warm over a low heat until melted. Simmer for 1–2 minutes, then sieve and put back in the pan (if the jam is a little thick, add a splash of water). Arrange the pineapple over the tart and brush with a thin layer of warm jam. Allow the jam to set before serving.

Serves 8	EASY		NUTRITIONAL INFORMATION	
	Preparation Time 1 hour, plus 50 minutes chilling	**Cooking Time** 55 minutes, plus cooling	**Per Serving** 648 calories, 36g fat (of which 17g saturates), 77g carbohydrate, 0.5g salt	Vegetarian

Mincemeat and Ricotta Tart

175g (6oz) plain flour, plus extra to dust
125g (4oz) butter, cut into cubes
25g (1oz) ground almonds
25g (1oz) caster sugar
1 large egg yolk

For the filling and topping
250g (9oz) ricotta cheese
25g (1oz) icing sugar, plus extra to dust
2 large egg yolks
3 tbsp double cream
700g (1½lb) vegetarian mincemeat
grated zest of 1 lemon
1 tbsp brandy or lemon juice
25g (1oz) glacé cherries, sliced
2 tbsp flaked almonds

1 To make the pastry, whiz the flour and the butter in a food processor until the mixture resembles fine crumbs. Add the ground almonds, sugar and egg yolk with 1 tbsp cold water. Pulse until the mixture just comes together. Knead lightly, wrap and chill for at least 30 minutes.

2 Roll out the pastry on a lightly floured surface and use to line a 10 x 33cm (4 x 13in) loose-based tin. Prick with a fork and chill for 30 minutes. Preheat the oven to 190°C (170°C fan oven) mark 5. Bake blind (see page 16). Cool for 15 minutes; reduce the oven temperature to 180°C (160°C fan oven) mark 4.

3 To make the filling, beat the ricotta with the icing sugar, egg yolks and cream. Spread over the pastry and bake for 20–25 minutes until lightly set.

4 Mix the mincemeat with the lemon zest and brandy or lemon juice, and spoon over the tart. Scatter the glacé cherries and almonds on top and bake for 20 minutes. Cool slightly, then dust with icing sugar.

Serves 8	EASY		NUTRITIONAL INFORMATION	
	Preparation Time 45 minutes, plus 1 hour chilling	**Cooking Time** about 1¼ hours, plus cooling	**Per Serving** 594 calories, 29g fat (of which 13g saturates), 78g carbohydrate, 0.3g salt	Vegetarian

Cook's Tip

Apple Sauce: put 300ml ($\frac{1}{2}$ pint) apple juice in a measuring jug. Mix 2 tbsp of the apple juice with 1 tbsp arrowroot to make a smooth paste. Pour the remaining apple juice into a small pan and bring to a gentle simmer. Add the arrowroot paste and continue to heat, stirring constantly, for 2–3 minutes until the sauce has thickened slightly.

Bramley Apple and Custard Tart

500g pack chilled shortcrust pastry

flour to dust

750g (1lb 11oz) Bramley apples, peeled, cored and roughly chopped

175g (6oz) golden caster sugar

400ml (14fl oz) double cream

1 cinnamon stick

3 large egg yolks, plus 1 large egg, beaten together

2 dessert apples to decorate

Apple Sauce (see Cook's Tip) to serve

1 Roll out the pastry on a lightly floured surface and use to line a 20.5cm (8in), 4cm (1½in) deep, loose-based fluted flan tin. Cover and chill for 1 hour. Preheat the oven to 180°C (160°C fan oven) mark 4. Bake the pastry case blind (see page 16).

2 Meanwhile, cook the apples with 2 tbsp water over a low heat until soft. Add 50g (2oz) sugar and beat to make a purée. Cool.

3 Put the cream in a pan with 50g (2oz) sugar and the cinnamon stick. Bring slowly to the boil, then remove from the heat and remove the cinnamon. Cool for 2–3 minutes then beat in the egg yolks and egg.

4 Reduce the oven temperature to 170°C (150°C fan oven) mark 3. Put the tart on a baking sheet, then spoon the apple purée over the pastry. Pour the cream mixture on top and bake for 1–1½ hours or until the custard is just set. Remove the tart from the oven, cool, then chill.

5 To decorate, preheat the grill. Cut the dessert apples into 5mm (¼in) thick slices and lay them on a lipped baking sheet. Sprinkle with 50g (2oz) sugar and grill for 4–5 minutes until caramelised, turn over and repeat on the other side, then cool. Decorate the tart with the apple slices and serve with Apple Sauce.

EASY		NUTRITIONAL INFORMATION		Serves
Preparation Time 30 minutes, plus 1 hour chilling	**Cooking Time** about 2 hours, plus cooling	**Per Serving** 472 calories, 32g fat (of which 15g saturates), 46g carbohydrate, 0.5g salt	Vegetarian	**12**

Try Something Different

Replace the apples with pears.

Caramelised Apple Tarts

1 pastry sheet from a 375g pack all-butter puff pastry
125g (4oz) white marzipan, chilled and coarsely grated
40g (1½oz) butter
4 crisp dessert apples, quartered, cored and sliced
juice of 1 large lemon
25g (1oz) demerara sugar
½ tsp ground mixed spice

1 Preheat the oven to 200°C (180°C fan oven) mark 6. Grease six 7.5cm (3in) tartlet tins. Roll out the pastry a little more thinly. Cut out six 12.5cm (5in) rounds of pastry, using a saucer as a guide. Line the tins and prick twice with a fork. Chill for 10 minutes.

2 Bake blind (see page 16). Sprinkle the marzipan over the pastry and bake for a further 5 minutes until the marzipan melts and the pastry is cooked.

3 Heat the butter in a large non-stick frying pan. Add the apples, lemon juice, sugar and mixed spice, and cook over a high heat for 5 minutes, turning the apples until just tender and most of the lemon juice has evaporated.

4 Pile the apples into the warm pastry cases, then put back in the oven for 2–3 minutes. Serve warm.

Serves	EASY		NUTRITIONAL INFORMATION	
6	**Preparation Time** 20 minutes, plus 10 minutes chilling	**Cooking Time** about 30 minutes	**Per Serving** 395 calories, 24g fat (of which 4g saturates), 45g carbohydrate, 0.6g salt	Vegetarian

Freezing Tip

Cool the tart completely in the tin. Wrap in foil and freeze for up to one month.
To use Remove from the freezer 12 hours before serving and thaw in the refrigerator.

Fruit and Walnut Tart

Sweet Shortcrust Pastry (see page 12), made with 225g (8oz) plain flour, 125g (4oz) butter, 2 tbsp golden icing sugar and 1 medium egg

For the filling
200g (7oz) clear honey

125g (4oz) unsalted butter, softened

125g (4oz) light muscovado sugar

3 medium eggs, beaten

grated zest and juice of 1 lemon

125g (4oz) walnuts, roughly chopped

125g (4oz) ready-to-eat dried apples and pears, roughly chopped, plus 3 dried pear slices to decorate

1 To make the filling, warm 175g (6oz) honey in a small pan over a low heat. Put the butter in a large bowl with the sugar and beat with an electric hand whisk until light and fluffy. Add the eggs, lemon zest and juice, walnuts, chopped apples and pears, and warm honey. Stir well and set aside.

2 Put the pastry between two sheets of greaseproof paper and roll out thinly. Peel off and discard the top sheet, then flip over and use the pastry to line a 23cm (9in) round or a 20.5cm (8in) square loose-based tin. Prick with a fork, cover with clingfilm and chill for 30 minutes. Preheat the oven to 180°C (160°C fan oven) mark 4. Bake the pastry case blind (see page 16).

3 Pour in the filling, and arrange the pear slices on top. Brush with the remaining honey.

4 Put the tart on a baking sheet, cover with foil and bake for 20 minutes. Remove the foil and bake for a further 25 minutes until golden brown. Serve cool.

EASY		NUTRITIONAL INFORMATION		Serves
Preparation Time 25 minutes, plus 1 hour chilling	**Cooking Time** 1 hour 5 minutes, plus cooling	**Per Serving** 646 calories, 40g fat (of which 18g saturates), 68g carbohydrate, 0.6g salt	Vegetarian	**8**

Mango Tartes Tatin

2 small ripe mangoes, peeled, the flesh cut away in one piece from each side of the stone
40g (1½oz) golden granulated sugar
40g (1½oz) butter
375g pack ready-rolled puff pastry

1 Preheat the oven to 220°C (200°C fan oven) mark 7. Slice each piece of mango along most of the length, so that the slices remain joined at the top.

2 Put the sugar into a large heavy-based frying pan. Heat very gently until it starts to dissolve and turn brown. Add 25g (1oz) butter and stir with a wooden spoon to make a caramel. Add the mango and toss gently to coat in caramel. Cook for 2–3 minutes, then remove from the heat.

3 Grease four 8cm (3¼in) tart tins with the remaining butter. Unroll the pastry and put the tins upside down on it. Press a rolling pin over the tins to stamp out four pastry rounds.

4 Put one mango piece, curved side down, into each tin, pressing it gently to fan out, then divide any remaining caramel among them. Top each tin with a pastry round. Bake for 20–25 minutes until the pastry is golden brown. To serve, turn out the tartlets on to plates, with the mango uppermost.

Serves 4	EASY		NUTRITIONAL INFORMATION	
	Preparation Time 30 minutes	**Cooking Time** 30 minutes, plus cooling	**Per Serving** 506 calories, 33g fat (of which 5g saturates), 56g carbohydrate, 0.9g salt	Vegetarian

Freezing Tip

To freeze Complete the recipe to the end of step 2, then cover, wrap and freeze.
To use Bake from frozen at 220°C (200°C fan oven) mark 7 for 40 minutes or until the pastry is golden. Complete the recipe.

Plum Tarte Tatin

75g (3oz) butter
125g (4oz) caster sugar
700g (1½lb) plums, halved and stoned
350g pack all-butter dessert pastry
flour to dust
crème fraîche or cream to serve

1 Melt the butter and sugar in a heavy-based frying pan. Cook, stirring, for 2–3 minutes until the sugar begins to turn light brown. Immediately add the plums and cook for 5 minutes or until the juices begin to run and the plums start to soften. Increase the heat and bubble until the juices are very syrupy. Lift the plums out of the pan into a 23cm (9in) shallow ovenproof dish or cake tin, with some of them cut-side up, and pour the juice over. Leave to cool.

2 On a lightly floured surface roll the pastry into a circle slightly larger than the dish and about 5mm (¼in) thick. Lay the pastry over the plums, tuck the edges down into the dish and make a few slits in the pastry with a knife to allow steam to escape. Chill for 20 minutes.

3 Preheat the oven to 220°C (200°C fan oven) mark 7. Bake for 20 minutes or until the pastry is golden. Cool for 5 minutes before carefully inverting on to a plate. Serve with crème fraîche or cream.

EASY		NUTRITIONAL INFORMATION		Serves
Preparation Time 30 minutes, plus 20 minutes chilling	**Cooking Time** 30 minutes, plus cooling	**Per Serving** 488 calories, 28g fat (of which 17g saturates), 59g carbohydrate, 0.5g salt	Vegetarian	**6**

Rhubarb and Orange Crumble Tart

200g (7oz) plain flour, plus extra to dust
125g (4oz) butter, cut into small pieces
25g (1oz) golden caster sugar
Elderflower Cream (see Cook's Tip) to serve

For the filling
550g (1¼lb) rhubarb, cut into 2.5cm (1in) pieces
50g (2oz) golden caster sugar
grated zest of 1 orange
juice of ½ an orange

For the crumble topping
50g (2oz) plain flour
25g (1oz) ground almonds
50g (2oz) light muscovado sugar
25g (1oz) butter, cut into small pieces

1 To make the pastry, whiz the flour, butter and sugar in a food processor until it resembles fine crumbs. (Alternatively, rub the butter into the flour in a large bowl by hand or using a pastry cutter until it resembles fine crumbs. Stir in the sugar.) Add 2 tbsp cold water and whiz briefly again, or stir with a fork, to form a soft pastry. Wrap the pastry in clingfilm and chill for at least 30 minutes.

2 Roll out the pastry on a lightly floured surface and use to line a 10 x 35.5cm (4 x 14in) loose-based tin, or a 23cm (9in) round loose-based tart tin. Chill for 30 minutes. Preheat the oven to 200°C (180°C fan oven) mark 6. Bake blind (see page 16).

3 Meanwhile, make the filling. Put the rhubarb, caster sugar, orange zest and juice in a pan and bring to the boil. Cook gently for 6–8 minutes until the rhubarb has just softened. Allow to cool.

4 To make the crumble topping, put the flour, almonds, muscovado sugar and butter into the food processor and whiz briefly until it resembles fine crumbs. (Alternatively, rub the butter into the flour in a bowl by hand or using a pastry cutter until it resembles fine crumbs. Stir in the almonds and sugar.)

5 Spoon the rhubarb filling into the pastry case and level the surface. Top with the crumble mixture and bake for 20 minutes until pale golden. Leave to cool slightly before serving with Elderflower Cream.

Cook's Tip

Elderflower Cream: put 300ml (½ pint) double cream, 1 tbsp golden icing sugar and 1 tbsp elderflower cordial in a bowl and whisk with an electric hand whisk until soft peaks form.

Serves 8	EASY		NUTRITIONAL INFORMATION	
	Preparation Time 25 minutes, plus 1 hour chilling	**Cooking Time** about 40 minutes, plus cooling	**Per Serving** 518 calories, 37g fat (of which 22g saturates), 45g carbohydrate, 0.3g salt	Vegetarian

Freezing Tip

To freeze Complete the recipe, wrap and freeze for up to one month.

To use Thaw overnight. Put on a baking sheet, cover loosely with foil and reheat at 200°C (180°C fan oven) mark 6 for 20 minutes.

Macadamia and Maple Tart

225g (8oz) macadamia nuts, halved

350g (12oz) ready-made shortcrust pastry, thawed if frozen

flour to dust

75g (3oz) butter, softened

75g (3oz) dark muscovado sugar

3 medium eggs, beaten

1 tsp cornflour

50ml (2fl oz) maple syrup, plus extra to drizzle

225ml (8fl oz) golden syrup

grated zest of 1 lemon and 2 tbsp lemon juice

1 tsp vanilla extract

1 Put the macadamia nuts on a baking sheet and toast under a hot grill until golden brown. Leave to cool.

2 Roll out the pastry on a lightly floured surface and use to line a 23cm (9in), 4cm (1½in) deep, loose-based tart tin, leaving the pastry hanging over the edges to prevent shrinkage. Prick with a fork, then freeze for 30 minutes. Preheat the oven to 200°C (180°C fan oven) mark 6.

3 Bake blind (see page 16). Using a sharp knife, trim the overhanging pastry to a neat edge.

4 Beat the butter with the sugar until pale and creamy, then gradually add the beaten egg and cornflour. Stir in all the remaining ingredients. The mixture will look curdled, but don't panic. Stir in the toasted nuts and pour into the cooked pastry case.

5 Bake for 35–40 minutes until the filling is just set. Leave to cool for 10 minutes before serving.

	EASY		NUTRITIONAL INFORMATION	
Serves 8	**Preparation Time** 15 minutes, plus 30 minutes freezing	**Cooking Time** about 40 minutes, plus cooling	**Per Serving** 608 calories, 38g fat (of which 11g saturates), 60g carbohydrate, 0.9g salt	Vegetarian